PAUL SEABRIDGE

# BUY
# BUILD
# SELL

The key to unleashing
your ambition and achieving
entrepreneurial success

# Rethink

First published in Great Britain in 2023 by Rethink Press (www.rethinkpress.com)

© Copyright Paul Seabridge

All rights reserved. No part of this publication may be reproduced, stored in or introduced into a retrieval system, or transmitted, in any form, or by any means (electronic, mechanical, photocopying, recording or otherwise) without the prior written permission of the publisher.

The right of Paul Seabridge to be identified as the author of this work has been asserted by him in accordance with the Copyright, Designs and Patents Act 1988.

This book is sold subject to the condition that it shall not, by way of trade or otherwise, be lent, resold, hired out, or otherwise circulated without the publisher's prior consent in any form of binding or cover other than that in which it is published and without a similar condition including this condition being imposed on the subsequent purchaser.

Every effort has been made to obtain the necessary permissions with reference to copyright material, both illustrative and quoted. We apologise for any omissions in this respect and will be pleased to make the appropriate acknowledgements in any future edition.

# Contents

| Introduction | 1 |
|---|---|
| **1 Entreprencurship** | **5** |
| An entrepreneur is born | 6 |
| Going it alone | 8 |
| Starting a business in a new industry | 9 |
| First mistakes | 11 |
| Moving forward | 15 |
| 'Shiny new thing' syndrome | 17 |
| Back to real estate – as a business owner | 18 |
| My first mentor | 20 |
| Summary | 24 |
| **2 Your Greatest Asset** | **25** |
| Attracting the right candidates | 27 |
| The holy trinity | 28 |
| The praise sandwich | 30 |

| | | |
|---|---|---|
| | Employee engagement | 33 |
| | Looking after employees | 35 |
| | Leadership | 38 |
| | The Three Cs | 40 |
| | Tiny noticeable things | 41 |
| | Make meetings productive and essential | 43 |
| | Chair | 49 |
| | Summary | 56 |
| 3 | **Reaching Customers** | **59** |
| | The Four Ps | 60 |
| | Market research | 62 |
| | Raising your profile | 68 |
| | Social media | 70 |
| | Becoming oversubscribed | 71 |
| | Sales | 74 |
| | The Five Cs | 77 |
| | Crossword selling | 82 |
| | Sales methodologies | 84 |
| | Sales process design | 86 |
| | Evaluating your sales process | 90 |
| | Common sales mistakes | 91 |
| | Selling complex solutions | 93 |
| | Negotiation | 97 |
| | Summary | 99 |

**4 Finance And Accounting For Non-Accountants**   **101**

   P&L   102
   Balance sheet   104
   Cashflow statement   107
   Economics: the basics   110
   Insolvency and restructuring   114
   Summary   118

**5 Productivity And Change**   **121**

   Workflow analysis   122
   Unfreeze, change and refreeze   126
   The House of Change   132
   A one-page strategy   136
   Summary   138

**6 Mergers And Acquisitions**   **139**

   Blowing the myth   140
   Buy, build, restore   141
   My biggest deal   143
   The M&A process   146
   Share Purchase Agreement (SPA) vs Asset Purchase Agreement (APA)   148
   Legal structures   151
   Going global   152
   Raising capital   153

|   |   |   |
|---|---|---|
|   | Structures used in acquisitions | 157 |
|   | Summary | 161 |
| 7 | **Capital Markets And Wealth** | **163** |
|   | IPO vs direct listing | 169 |
|   | SPAC | 172 |
|   | Wealth | 176 |
|   | Selling a company | 179 |
|   | Tax and citizenship | 181 |
|   | Summary | 182 |
| 8 | **The Way Forward** | **183** |
|   | Real estate investing | 183 |
|   | KPIs | 184 |
|   | Habits and actions | 186 |
|   | Making it | 187 |

**Acknowledgements**     **189**

**The Author**     **191**

# Introduction

Successful entrepreneur James Caan once said, 'Observe the masses and do the opposite.'[1] That is what I have done. I am in the 1% that doesn't see work as a means to a pension that won't give me what I want. I see my work as my life – what I enjoy doing, which has the helpful by-product of creating wealth, which gives me the luxury of choosing to live where and how I want. With this book, I want to help you do the same.

In 2003, I acquired my first business with no money down. One year later, I sold it, using the capital to reinvest in a new venture – my own start-up business in

---

1 J Caan, 'Best Advice: Observe the masses, do the opposite', LinkedIn (5 February 2015) www.linkedin.com/pulse/best-advice-observe-masses-do-opposite-james-caan-cbe

an industry in which I had absolutely no experience. What a risk. Twice, the business nearly went belly up before I managed to put it on a successful trajectory. Since then, I have bought, sold, merged and invested in over eighty companies in twenty-six different industries across nine countries, amounting to more than $0.5bn worth of revenue. My current investments cover organisations employing over 1,000 staff in several countries. My success isn't because I went to a top university, or knew someone who could make the right introductions. Quite the opposite.

A common trait among entrepreneurs is a dislike of following rules, preferring instead to make their own, particularly when they identify a more effective way of working. With this in mind, in 2001 I told my parents that I was going for an interview for a weekend job at an estate agent, which I'd fit in while completing my studies. Only after receiving the job offer did I admit I was quitting school to work. I knew that gaining experience in the real world would be better for me than classroom learning. Thankfully, my parents were supportive. I worked hard and soon became the company's best salesperson. Within a year I was given the opportunity to run my own team and office. I quickly deployed my skills and showed my colleagues how to perform better, turning the office around from making a loss to record profits within twelve months.

My journey in business has been a wild ride – extreme highs, extreme lows and a whole lot of fun in between.

## INTRODUCTION

One thing that has helped me is having mentors – someone who has been there, done it and got the T-shirt. Someone to learn from. Some mentors can be real people you connect with directly, others indirectly. For me, learning from successful entrepreneurs, reading their books and consuming their content has been hugely helpful. Now I want to share my experiences with aspiring entrepreneurs and business owners so that you can avoid a whole lot of heartache and mistakes. Don't get me wrong. I have no regrets. My experiences have shaped me as a businessperson, investor and human being – I'd like others to benefit from those experiences. We are only on this earth once; we have one shot to make it.

In my view, 99% of the Western world are taught to follow the same system. This is what sets me and the rest of the 1% apart. We finish school, some of us go to college, some of us head for university (which now costs on average £50,000, not including living costs). There's an argument that if you get a university education you have a better chance of a good career and will earn more over your lifetime than if you don't. You then work for forty years before retiring on a pension that, given the cost of living these days, is unlikely to pay the bills so you downgrade to a simpler life, then you die.

Well, f*** that. Life is for living. Live every day as if it's your last, enjoy it, embrace it, have no regrets. Money does not buy happiness but it does allow you to make

3

choices that can make you happy. I'd rather be rich and unhappy than poor and unhappy.

*Buy, Build, Sell* is an accessible and informative guide that follows my journey to buying my first business and starting my first company. I talk about people, my core learnings along the way, the levers to pull to improve performance, mergers and acquisitions – the only way I know to double or triple your business and create significant wealth in a single afternoon – and finally the realities of wealth, tax and planning for the future.

In this book, you'll discover my journey from faking it to making it, from being broke to becoming a multi-millionaire entrepreneur and the experiences I've had along the way. But this book is also about you: your business, your potential, your future. Whether you're a young entrepreneur intent on propelling your business forward, or a seasoned business owner looking to sell and move on, *Buy, Build, Sell* will demonstrate how you can achieve your goals.

ONE
# Entrepreneurship

Many people would describe themselves as an entrepreneur. An entrepreneur is essentially a person who founds a business (often multiple businesses); this typically involves a financial risk and they usually hope to turn a profit. But most 'entrepreneurs' are faking it. They present themselves as a business owner, or are some smart kid on YouTube making money as an influencer or selling stuff online, but they are not truly entrepreneurial.

Being an entrepreneur is probably one of the toughest paths you can follow. According to the US Small Business Administration, 95% of business start-ups fail within the first five years.[2] The statistics are similar

---

2   B Moriarty, 'Top 5 reasons why small businesses fail', Star Micronics (4 September 2018), https://starmicronics.com/blog/top-5-reasons-why-small-businesses-fail

in most Western countries. I can think of countless people who have started a business and failed, including world famous entrepreneurs such as Virgin founder Richard Branson, Henry Ford of The Ford Motor Company and Walt Disney.[3] Failure is OK, as long as you learn from your mistakes. Even now I make mistakes. There are times when I've lost or failed but these have shaped me and helped me become a better human and a more experienced operator. Even so, ideally you will get to a place where you win more than you lose.

It's a bit like cooking. When you first start cooking, you may not add enough seasoning, or overlook a garnish. As a result, the food may be bland or not look as you want it to. But you learn, and the next time you attempt that dish, you apply your experience and get a different result. Business is no different. Though some things, like classic dishes, are tried and tested and work every time, you have to refine your technique and add your own twist, and to really excel you must constantly change, adapt and learn.

## An entrepreneur is born

I was born in England. My father first worked in law enforcement then moved into the legal profession. My mother had a successful career in telecommunications

---

3   M Dunlop, 'Went broke, now worth millions', Incomediary.com (no date), www.incomediary.com/went-bankrupt-now-worth-millions

before taking time out to have children. When my brother and I were pre-school age, my mum volunteered at a local playgroup, eventually taking on a part-time role that fit around family life. When the owner of that business decided to retire, my mum took the opportunity to buy it. Before long, she had transformed the playgroup into a thriving nursery school. This is where my interest in business first began.

Due to their busy lives, my parents insisted that on Friday evenings it was the time that we all gathered around the dining table to share our news. On many of these occasions we focused on mum's business and the challenges she faced, all chipping in to offer solutions. It was hugely successful as a nursery, but as a business it was treading water, it wasn't exactly losing money but it wasn't making any either. Some months my mother would forfeit a wage to ensure she had sufficient money to pay the staff and bills. My mum is brilliant with kids and from an educational point of view this nursery was the best. Ofsted, the UK inspectorate of educational establishments, gave her an 'Outstanding' rating (the best possible) several times.

But from a business point of view, there were sleepless nights. I thought I could fix this so I went to my mother with an offer: I would take over the business, guarantee she was paid a monthly wage and take away from her the challenges that kept her awake. To my surprise, she agreed. We streamlined the staffing structure and built a senior team that ensured the organisation operated successfully, not just as a nursery but as a business. I was still working as an estate agent and this was my first foray into running a business for myself, and laid the foundations for my future success. But before we get into the detail of the different businesses I've founded, bought and been involved in, we need to rewind a bit.

## Going it alone

By 2004 I was thriving in my estate agency job and earning good money but the company I worked for was old-fashioned. The business had been treading water; I turned one office around and was asked to do the same in other parts of the company. This was when I decided that there was more to life than being an employee and making money for someone else. I thought, I have proven I can do it in real estate. I'd proven already as a nineteen year old, who knew nothing about kids and parenting, that I could turn around a nursery by running the business side of things complemented by my mum in charge of the operations. So I decided I wanted to start my own business, I just wasn't sure what. It took me five months to work that out before I quit my job and set out on my own. Before I tell you about that crazy period, to give you context as to how I came up with my first start-up idea, I must take you back to the real estate job.

In my role, I had made record profits. It wasn't rocket science. Before I arrived, there was no strategy, no targets, no training, no structure, no vision. The first thing I did was recruit good people. I needed better, smarter, more talented, experienced people. I set about identifying who was good in the competition and figuring out why. I would phone them up, invite them for a-nothing-ventured-nothing-gained coffee and a chat, where I would get to know them and work out how I was going to get them to work for me instead.

I started to research the recruitment marketplace. Back then, there was only one national real estate recruiter and several smaller regional players, most focusing on London, which has a fierce real estate market. I spotted a niche – I could headhunt real estate professionals and supply them to firms that were recruiting. This was when the idea for my first business was born.

## Starting a business in a new industry

According to the Recruitment and Employment Confederation, in 2004 the UK recruitment industry was worth £24bn and growing at a rate of 7%; globally it was worth $0.5tr. There were few barriers to entry and all anyone needed was a phone, a website and a laptop and they could start a business in this space. Which is exactly what I did.

I spent several months designing a business plan: I would headhunt people at the top of their game and supply them to real estate companies that wanted talented people. I would target all the main corporate agents and larger regional players and then scale the business by taking on more recruitment consultants to cover a particular niche or region. Having worked in the industry, I had an edge – I understood the challenges these companies were facing in hiring great people.

For the rest of the summer, I worked on marketing and built the financial forecasts. Over the years I've learned a lot about finance and accounting, but back then I knew very little. My rather optimistic forecast showed that in the first year my company would be making £500k revenue which, by year five, would have grown to £50m. I have since learned that anyone can make figures and forecasts look as good or as bad as they want. Mine was purely focused on showing strong growth, without consideration of the 'how'. My first mistake.

During a family holiday with my parents and brother to France, each morning I worked on my website and business plan and in the afternoons enjoyed the French countryside and beaches with my brother. It was on this holiday that I shared with him, having not yet mentioned it to anyone, that I was planning to quit my well-paid job with good future prospects and set up my own business in a sector in which I had absolutely no experience. Of course he supported me, as did my parents, but that's the thing with friends and family. Your biggest fans will always be positive and tell you what you want to hear. At this point, I should have sought out a mentor from the recruitment industry, someone who could have warned me of all the mistakes I was about to make.

## First mistakes

I returned from holiday in August 2004 and handed in my notice. On my last day I returned my company car and went to pick up the new car I had purchased – a brand new black BMW 3 Series, a car I had always wanted. As a new entrepreneur, I thought I needed a flashy vehicle like all the people I aspired to. Of course, with hindsight I know I would have been better investing that money in training and a mentor and buying that car only once I'd made it.

My next mistake was believing that being a new start-up business would prevent me from securing a lease on premises, because of a lack of credit rating. Instead, I signed up to a serviced office provider which proved to be ridiculously expensive. I then hired a good real estate agent – young, successful and up and coming – bought him a shiny BMW too and paid him a hefty salary. I sold the nursery (to another employee with my mum supposedly retiring) and invested the profits plus all my savings from my employment in my business.

The market operated like most recruitment marketplaces: recruiters advertised to find staff, interviewed potential candidates and then threw them at employers in a big mail-out in the hope that someone would stick. This was my opportunity. My candidates would be handpicked; they would be better and more experienced, more successful, not actively looking for a job. I thought this meant I could charge a premium. Before long I spotted the flaw in this model: the process I proposed was incredibly time consuming. I scrapped my business plan and decided to follow my competition – I advertised for staff. Within a couple of weeks we had hundreds of candidates and started throwing CVs at employers hoping some would be successful. But the feedback from interviews was not great and we quickly gained a reputation for being no different to our competition.

If someone is successful in their job, they are probably well paid and have good future prospects there, so why would they be looking for something else? Generally, the candidates we attracted through our advertising were not the best, they needed a new role and were either under pressure or not performing – hardly the best people to recruit.

Nevertheless, a placement within the first month meant our first revenue. We'd managed to place one of the candidates we'd advertised for, so we thought maybe the model did work, we just needed to up the volume. I secured that first placement by attending a networking event where I met a property investor/landlord and discovered that he, like me, had decided to set up a business with no industry experience. He told me he wanted to recruit a manager to run the day-to-day. I advertised and a candidate applied. He had a credible CV showing twenty-five years' experience as a manager, albeit in a different location. He talked the talk and after two interviews was offered the job. I sent in my invoice and was paid. It later turned out that the candidate had been about to be let go from his previous job for poor performance and, after six months working for my client, they quickly realised he wasn't as good as his CV suggested and he was fired.

Meanwhile, we were rapidly burning through everything that had been invested. I thought there had to be a better way. I started looking into buying a recruitment franchise – I thought a franchise would give me training in tried-and-tested methods that could put me on the right track. In the end, I didn't buy a franchise but the process did lead me to a successful entrepreneur who ran a multimillion-pound recruitment business. He offered to train me and my team at his office in Lancashire, teaching me how to headhunt and how to run this kind of business properly.

I had roped my mother and brother in to help at this point and left them to man the office while I and my new manager did the training. After just one day I told them to close the office and join us so they too could benefit from what we were learning. The penny had dropped; I could see the processes we had to put in place to make the business successful. I also realised I needed to cut costs.

I left the serviced office and worked from the back bedroom of my parents' house. Our home became recruitment headquarters. Three months later, we started placing excellent quality candidates and began to make some money. This led me to begin recruiting for one of the major independent real estate businesses in the UK. We were invited to their head office in the south of England, pitched to the managing director and came away with a string of new roles to recruit. They ended up becoming one of our best clients.

Before long, however, itchy feet indicated my need to expand. Nine months in, you would have thought I'd have learned from my mistakes, but no. I signed a lease on an office and filled it with new recruits. Instead of applying my new headhunting knowledge and experience to my own business, I hired hungry salespeople in the hope I could train them up to be good recruiters. Half worked out, half didn't.

We then went through two years of switching premises, making money, reinvesting in recruiters who burned through our cash in wages with nothing to show for it. It took three years to refine the model to one that worked.

## Moving forward

In 2007, before the financial crash, we had started to gain a good reputation and had a steady flow of great clients who paid top whack to attract talent and settled our fees on time. I thought we could expand this into other areas associated with real estate, such as the mortgages, finance and legal. I also saw a niche for RPO (recruitment process outsourcing). James Caan, an entrepreneur who inspired me, is founder of Alexander Mann, the first RPO business in the UK, which he grew and sold, making him a multimillionaire. I had read James' books and followed him online. I thought RPO was something we could do in the real estate and finance industry.

I hired an ex-Fortune 500 executive with a background in BPO (business process outsourcing), offering him a share in the new venture, and we set about travelling the length and breadth of the country pitching the model to our clients. The benefits to the client if they let us do all of their recruitment would be a lower cost to them, they would improve their time to hire (productivity) and hire better people. For us, it was long-term, contracted, recurring and profitable revenue.

We pitched our main client, an organisation with about 2,000 staff, and signed them up on a six-figure contract. We were helping them hire twenty to thirty people every month and had a whole team working on it. Our model was to charge a monthly retainer, then we added bonuses on top for each hire and, if we improved the time to hire, we would earn more money. This was great for cashflow, due to guaranteed long-term contracted cash coming in, unlike headhunting where cashflow is only as good as last week's sales figures. The retainers paid the fixed costs and the contract bonuses were our profits.

I ended up pitching FTSE 250 companies in the finance and real estate space. One was a foreign bank that had just acquired several UK banks and wanted to build out their corporate banking arm. They had hired the CEO of one of the UK's largest banks to do this and his remit was to build the biggest corporate bank in the UK from pretty much no market share. He wanted to hire 300 corporate bankers to cover the UK. I sat in the boardroom of one of the world's biggest banks with their CEO and COO and pitched our RPO model. For a fixed price we would hire all 300 of his corporate bankers.

I was loving it. We were placing high-level candidates, I was meeting interesting people and I felt at this point that we were on a path to greatness. Then, in 2008, the financial crisis hit. Nevertheless, we doubled our sales in 2009. If we hadn't diversified into RPO and created long-term regular cashflow I know we would have gone bust, as most people stopped recruiting or scaled back significantly. We grew because we were offering those that were still recruiting a better value and more effective way to recruit the best talent.

## 'Shiny new thing' syndrome

Soon, though, boredom set in. Entrepreneurs are renowned for flitting from one project to the next, it's what I call 'shiny new thing' syndrome. I had gone from enjoying chasing the deal and making those placements, to simply managing a team of people. All I talked about was time to hire, KPIs (key persons of interest), how many vacancies were live, and fill rates. For me, it had become a different business.

One of the big lessons I learned here was that, when you fall out of love with a business, it's time to get out. When you are no longer passionate, you lose focus and the business declines. I negotiated my exit and ended up going to work for one of my clients to run their real estate division in London. In twelve months, I took the division (one of thirteen in the company) from near the bottom to the second most profitable. We tripled our profits in that year by doing all the stuff I had done previously – which you will learn about in the coming chapters.

I knew, though, that this was not a long-term thing. Living in the northwest meant getting up early on Monday morning to make the two-hour train journey to London, working crazy long hours Monday to Thursday and living out of a suitcase in hotel rooms, before catching an evening train back home from work on Fridays. This took its toll on me and I knew it wasn't sustainable, even though the money was good. More importantly though, working for and making money for someone else was just not my style. I gave it just over a year then resigned and went back to working for myself. I've not had a job since.

## Back to real estate – as a business owner

Before I bought my next business I decided to venture into the start-up space again, setting up a specialist headhunting business but this time for the recruitment industry. You read that right – recruitment-to-recruitment (or rec2rec, as it's more commonly known) is a booming industry in which recruiters are paid to find recruiters.

I rented cheap offices and hired a team of four and within three weeks we'd made our first placement and our first revenue. At this point, I had the opportunity to acquire my second business. I had heard that the real estate company where I worked before I left to start up my recruitment business in 2004 was struggling. The owner had come out of retirement in the south of France because the financial crisis had decimated the business. He had to take out a hefty bank loan to pay significant redundancy costs and close offices so the business could survive. I looked up the accounts at Companies House (the registry of companies in the UK where their financial data is published) and it was clear that things were not going well. I wrote to the owner at his home address explaining what I had been up to since leaving his employment and expressing my interest in buying his business. He came to see me a few days later. A series of meetings ensued and a deal was agreed.

At this point, I made another mistake: using my own cash to buy a business that was struggling. I should have negotiated taking a percentage stake in the business in return for my expertise to help him turn it around and then exit together. But while I was experienced in turning around real estate businesses (I'd done this with three by this point) and had a good grounding in how to run a business and manage large teams, I was not experienced in mergers and acquisitions. I used my own capital (and that of friends and family) to make a down payment to acquire the business – taking on its debt too – with a deferred note to pay the rest over a three-year period.

On day one I again roped in my mother and brother and we went around all the offices and departments to meet the staff. It was similar to 2003, just with a lot of debt to sort out – no vision, no strategy, no KPIs and no structure. In the first few weeks we made some pretty tough decisions, including redundancies. Laying off hard-working staff is never a pleasant task, anyone who says they enjoy that is either lying or heartless. But we made those decisions for the sake of the business. Had we not removed costs, the business would not have survived. I spent three years turning things around, going from substantial debt to six-figure profits. We twice used insolvency to restructure the business, hiving off the good parts from the bad and putting it on the straight and narrow. Some things worked, some didn't.

I again realised that while we had been successful, I was working crazy hours and didn't have the time to enjoy the fruits of my labour. After exiting the business, I became involved in a few start-up ventures before deciding to go into mergers and acquisitions full time. Mergers and acquisitions (M&A) was when I had my paradigm shift moment – in how to really scale a business significantly, literally overnight.

## My first mentor in M&A

I have already touched on the importance of mentors and, at this point in my business life, I had learned a valuable lesson: if you are going to become a success or an expert in a particular field, you need to find a mentor.

On researching mergers and acquisitions I came across Jeremy Harbour. Jeremy is a global entrepreneur and a master deal maker. He's done hundreds of deals, including taking several companies public. He also teaches people how to do mergers and acquisitions properly. By now I was in the second decade of my business career. Having completed several deals myself I was keen to further my knowledge in mergers and acquisitions (M&A), so I flew out to Majorca where he was based and joined the Harbour Club –a global community of fellow dealmakers. Jeremy became one of the best mentors I have ever worked with. I have since gone on to do deals with him and he continues to be a mentor and a good friend.

Jeremy teaches mergers and acquisitions to people around the world. While there are many people selling M&A programmes, these tend just to be good marketers who haven't done any deals themselves. But Jeremy is the real deal. Back in the 1990s, Jeremy ran a successful telecoms business and would constantly be pitched by competitors wanting to buy his company. All these potential buyers had one thing in common – none of them had any money. This is when the penny dropped. Instead of being a seller, Jeremy became a buyer with no money.

Until meeting Jeremy Harbour I thought that in order to buy a business you needed real money. You don't. Like I did, you might think that when you buy a business, the owner puts it up for sale with an asking price, negotiates with the buyers and walks away with the cash. In fact, while businesses do sell for 'real money', a lot don't.

Jeremy teaches various different 'no money down' strategies you can use to acquire multimillion-pound businesses. I can testify that they work because I've used them. Since that first time, I have not invested any of my own capital into acquisitions. You may think this strange, but later in the book we'll look at how you raise the capital needed to do deals. You may wonder, particularly if you are a business owner thinking of selling, why would you sell a business to someone who isn't putting any money in? This is just how it is done. The biggest business transaction in the UK in 2021 was when ASDA (a major UK supermarket) was sold by its US parent, Walmart, in a $10bn deal – most of which was not the buyer's own money but came from a contingent of banks.[4]

Since 2015 I have done more than eighty transactions across twenty-six industries in nine different countries. In the vast majority of these I acquired well-run, profitable, established businesses and then brought in my own team and expertise to make them bigger and better – then we'd exit. For those seeking wealth creation, this kind of deal is the single biggest opportunity there is. Up to 2015 I had bought and sold a few

---

4  B King, 'Asda: How to buy a £6.8bn supermarket for £780m', BBC News (16 February 2021) www.bbc.com/news/business-56085128

businesses and started a few more. Once established, I earned good money – but the more you earn, the more you spend. Most people live to their means; more income just means driving better cars, buying a bigger house, taking more exotic holidays, etc. What is life-changing is the capital event – the sale or disposal of a company or its assets – you get off the back of selling a business. While there are some anomalies, most businesses sell for a multiple of profit. This means that, if you buy a business making £250k a year profit for, say, a multiple of three, then spend two years improving that business to make £400k profit, and sell for a multiple of three or four, you make a decent capital event. You then reinvest these capital events to create a passive income stream. More on that later.

I have sold dozens of businesses for five, six, seven and even eight figures. My time is now spent finding and doing deals. I have homes in different countries and I live in southern Europe for most of the year enjoying a Mediterranean lifestyle. The view from my office is of the sun shining down on the sea. Most of my work is done remotely over Zoom, and I have a brilliant team of people around the world who focus on finding and doing deals and a highly experienced executive team who take care of operations and strategy in the businesses we buy or invest in. This is not hard to achieve. In the coming chapters, I will explain how I have assembled my team and how we operate.

## Summary

Being a successful entrepreneur is about more than just you. Having the right (and the best) people in the right places doing the right things is crucial. Mentors are hugely beneficial and can help you avoid costly mistakes – though it's likely you will still make mistakes along the way. Learn from these. You also need great sales and marketing and rigorous financial control, which we'll go into more detail on later in this book. Get those things right and you are on the right path. Get just one of them wrong and you will likely join the 95% of failed start-ups. Business success may not look how you thought it would – work out what success looks like for you and then begin to build it.

## TWO
# Your Greatest Asset

CEOs and senior executives will often espouse the value and importance of employees. 'Our people are our greatest asset' is a well-worn and now somewhat clichéd expression but the results for firms that 'walk the walk' are measurable; recruitment, retention (reduced staff turnover), staff development and succession all feed into top-line sales and bottom-line profitability.

I spent six years in my headhunting business preaching to clients that, 'Your business is only as good as your people; hire better people for a better business, then retain them.' This is still what I preach to the senior executives running my businesses today. Look after your workforce and they will look after your clients.

When I build new teams, I engage our own internal headhunters to support me in finding the best. When starting or acquiring a business, the first thing to focus on is getting the right people in the right places doing the right things. Initially, I write a long list of who I need and where I will find that talent – this is anything from company names (competitors) to individuals, after researching the market to identify the key players. Once I have a list I contact each individual, explain who I am, why I want to talk to them, assure them of confidentiality and invite them for a coffee and a chat.

I now have a team that supports recruitment across our group of companies, but when it was just me doing the hiring, I would write to people. Here is an example of how I would pitch an opportunity:

*Hi <name>*

*Please excuse the direct approach. My name is Paul Seabridge. I am the CEO of Opulentia Capital and we have recently acquired a £15m turnover logistics business. The existing owner is due to retire and we are looking to hire a top-class MD to take this business from £15m to £100m in five years. I appreciate you are probably quite happy in your current role and have not thought about moving elsewhere – good people never do because they are successful, earn well and have a bright future. However, I would welcome the opportunity to discuss this with you, confidentially, on a nothing-ventured-nothing-gained informal basis, perhaps over a coffee. When would be convenient to call?*

First lesson: hire the best people. If people are the organisation's greatest asset, it is vital to recruit the right ones. While all employees are, of course, important, it is the top talent that make the biggest difference to organisational success and it is here that you should focus.

## Attracting the right candidates

A good starting point, and something often missed in SMEs (small and medium enterprises), is to ask yourself why people would want to come and work for you. What is the business's USP? Does it have a compelling story? A little while ago I heard the story of a small business in the technology industry. It was so inspirational that we captured what had made the entrepreneur set up the business and what he was passionate about in a presentation, which was later used as part of the recruitment interview process.

Secondly, it is important to define the role: job description, person specification or role profile. What do you want this person to do?

Next, you want to attract people to apply, to give you a pool of suitable talent from which you can recruit. Small businesses tend to recruit people they already know but it is important to look beyond these people, as they might not have the skills and experience needed for the role. Once you have recruited a pool of potential candidates, you need to select the most suitable, the best of these. But how do you know who that is?

## The holy trinity

The most widely used recruitment and selection tool is referred to as the 'holy trinity', which consists of:

- CV
- Interview
- References

At the recruitment and selection stage we can (but often don't) consider conducting some sort of assessment or testing. Assessment centres can be useful for certain cohorts of employees, such as graduate entrants or those identified as having potential for a management development programme. This is your opportunity to seek evidence of past behaviour that can be used to predict future performance. Traditional interviews are poor predictors. The structured or behavioural event interview, where candidates are asked to discuss specific situations, the tasks and actions they undertook and what the results were, are more likely to be good predictors of future performance.

References are not always followed up but they ought to be. I find that people tend to be more open on the phone and will give you more than just the basic confirmation that the person was employed in a particular role for a certain period of time. For the potential employer, the key question to ask is: 'Would you re-employ this person?'

Most employers recruit candidates who have done the same job for a direct competitor, to mitigate risk in hiring. But some organisations think differently and instead of focusing on skills, they hire based on attitude, knowing they can upskill the 'right' people. When I was recruiting for a global electronics company, I found their approach was refreshing: they believed that anyone could do any job.

Once engaged, it may be possible to have the applicant undertake a work trial. I would recommend a probationary period of three to six months, after which measurable objectives for employees should be agreed with regular one-to-one check-ins to monitor progress. This also helps hugely with retention, another important consideration as, once you have the right and the best people, it's critical that you keep hold of them.

## The praise sandwich

I am a strong believer that, as a leader or manager, you should always strive to help your team members improve. A great way to do this is through feedback and coaching. I have a method for this, used and refined over twenty years, which I have found to be effective. I call it the praise sandwich. You have two pieces of bread with a filling in the middle. The two pieces of bread are the positive feedback you want to deliver; the filling is the not so good part that the employee needs to change.

The way you deliver that feedback is also important. If I said to you, 'You are great at this, not very good at that, but really good at this', I am simply telling you my feedback. This is not productive. Instead, you want to get the person receiving the feedback to do most of the talking; you want *them* to tell *you* what they're doing well and not so well.

For instance, instead of saying, 'That call wasn't good', I might ask, 'How do you think that call went?' Or, 'If you were to do things differently next time, what would you change?' If they struggle to say what you need them to say, you can probe further. 'When you said this to the customer, how did they respond? How do you think they perceived that? Would you word it differently next time? What would you say?'

I try to have 70% of the feedback focusing on three positive things that you appreciate and want them to keep doing, and 30% focused on development. Roughly speaking:

- The first piece of bread equates to 50% of the conversation, talking about the positives
- The filling is 30% of the conversation, speaking about the areas for improvement
- The second piece of bread is the final 20% of the conversation, recapping the positives

Make sure you signpost each section. For instance, 'In summary, I need you to keep doing XYZ. Now let's talk about the areas you think could be improved/changed. So next time, you will do XYZ.' Be sure to always circle back and finish on a positive.

You can use this type of feedback to improve processes/methods and behaviour. For example, if you had an employee turning up late for work you could have a conversation like this:

'What time did you arrive to work this morning?' (Late)

'Why did you not arrive at the start time?' (Overslept)

'How can you ensure you arrive for work on time?' (Set the alarm clock earlier)

With this way of delivering feedback, you get the team member to answer probing questions so that they identify the feedback themselves without you having to state it for them. The reason you want to get the person to tell *you* what they're doing and what they need to change, is that no one likes being told off or told what to do. A level of emotional intelligence is required, to show empathy towards all members of your organisation and ensure they feel valued within the business. Using kind language and balancing out any criticism with positive comments is important to maintain a consistent level of positivity.

Coaching is leading from the front and showing an individual what to do. When coaching someone, I always focus the session on a particular topic. Back when I hired trainee recruiters, I would make sales calls with them and show them how I did it. Then I would ask them to make a call while I observed, giving feedback afterwards. Coaching also involves setting goals and taking actions. It is a great way to help people develop skill sets and grow their competence within a business, especially if the coach/ mentor has specific and relevant expertise in an area of knowledge. This is one of the more direct ways in which a leader in the business can help to develop the expertise and skill sets of the team.

## Employee engagement

This is something I talk about a lot in the businesses I get involved in. I have already emphasised the importance of hiring and retaining the best people. It is not uncommon, particularly in family-run businesses, for staff turnover to be a little high. Many family businesses tend to function as lifestyle businesses. They provide the owner with a good lifestyle – nice car, nice home, holiday home, etc. In this context, an ambitious employee looking for growth opportunities may not be encouraged or supported to grow the business because this challenges the status quo and puts the owner's lifestyle at risk. They are content with their lot – and what if the plans fail? This lack of interest in growth and progress can have a detrimental impact on employee engagement, which is key to retention, and could undo all your hard work in the recruitment stage.

The first thing we look at when we acquire a business is employee engagement. To do this, we conduct a survey asking for employees' opinions and feedback, which we analyse and then we address any areas where improvement is needed. This is like internal market research. If you ask your customers for their opinions you will find opportunities for improvement and growth. It's the same with employees; if you ask them what they do and don't like, what they would change, what ideas they have for the business, you can uncover some pretty powerful stuff to act on.

For example, working with a well-established family business we wanted to take a snapshot of how people felt about working for the company, which was undergoing a process of transformation. We conducted an anonymous employee engagement survey, in which staff were encouraged to highlight any concerns and help identify where the business could improve. The survey results revealed how people truly felt about their job and the company. As a result, the managing director implemented a number of initiatives, including a Continuous Improvement Circle, where small groups of employees met, identified and agreed on how issues could be addressed and then created an improvement plan. As customer service improved, cost savings were achieved.

In another business we took over we identified that some of the workforce were really unhappy as part of their role meant working outside, which was fine in the summer but not in the colder winter months. We provided them with warmer workwear and built an outdoor workshop that kept the elements at bay, which made a huge difference. If we hadn't asked, we wouldn't have known why so many staff had been leaving and why sickness absence was so much higher in the winter. What may seem obvious to one person sometimes isn't to another – seeking feedback and measuring and improving employee engagement is a sure fire way to improve a business. This is closely related to my next point, which is about the importance of looking after your employees.

## Looking after employees

Why do people work? Some time ago I asked a class of young adults, 'Why do people work?' They all shouted, 'Money'. Of course, money is important. Money enables people to pay for their essential material and physiological needs in life, including food and shelter. But work can also provide a sense of belonging and opportunities for personal growth, which is less easy to understand in transactional terms. Certain things have to be right in the work environment, or they will cause job dissatisfaction; these things are:

- Salary and benefits
- Job security
- Work environment
- Work policies
- Supervisory practices
- Company policies and administration
- Company reputation

On the other hand, positive motivators include:

- Achievement
- Recognition of accomplishments
- Opportunities for advancement
- Creativity

- Variety
- Independence
- Interesting work
- Responsibility
- Personal development
- Interpersonal relationships
- Status

But how do we implement and measure these things? In my experience, smaller firms often don't know what good HR looks like, business administration not being one of their core competencies. Someone who has built a business based on their own skill set – perhaps they are a good carpenter – often has little understanding of people management and development. A good starting point is to conduct an HR audit at the firm to find out what they have in place and identify any gaps or possible causes of job dissatisfaction. We often find that the basics are missing: no contracts of employment, no HR policies and procedures or Employee Handbook, lack of internal record keeping, no e-HR system. An HR audit of a wealth management company recently revealed the need to update some HR policies and procedures (including those relating to maternity and paternity leave) and the need to implement an appraisal and performance management process. People want to achieve at work and need to be recognised for their achievements and accomplishments. In a different firm, a commercial cleaning company with 200 staff, we conducted a salary survey as the managing director was concerned that salaries and rewards were not in line with the market. A detailed analysis of management roles compared to direct competitors revealed that some of the jobs were below the upper quartile level that the business strategy had identified as necessary to recruit and retain top talent.

Once the causes of job dissatisfaction have been addressed, it's time to consider the positive motivators. We know that motivated and committed employees who feel valued give their best. Committed and motivated employees behave differently. They work hard and are prepared to go the extra mile. In short, they are more productive. This can be a real differentiator and a source of competitive advantage. When was the last time you received great customer service in a shop? How likely are you to go back or recommend that business to others?

For example, a national care group I worked with was growing rapidly through acquisitions but recruiting and retaining staff was difficult. We wanted to change the employees' mindset from having a job with the company to having a career. We developed a career framework that identified the competencies necessary for care workers and what was then needed to progress to team leader or manager. This enabled individuals to develop and progress, which improved retention and helped to attract potential employees.

The employment market these days is difficult, and recent events including the Covid-19 pandemic have highlighted the importance of people and pushed HR up the agenda for many organisations. Addressing job dissatisfaction and enabling positive motivators for employees at work provides firms with a sustainable competitive advantage where it's people that make the difference.

## Leadership

I have had the privilege of working with some exceptional people over my twenty-two years in business. The most successful senior executives I have worked with have all had one thing in common – they were all exceptional leaders. But what is good leadership and how do you become a better leader?

People have different leadership styles and what may suit one person won't suit another. For me, a great leader is someone who commands attention and respect. When they walk into a room, they light it up; they have charisma and energy but they also know how to come up with a strategy and a vision for a company or department and how to get everyone motivated to deliver it. They are fair but firm. They will roll their sleeves up and, whether they are talking to a worker on the shop floor, a board executive or an important customer, they can communicate at all levels and understand how to solve problems and overcome challenges. They know how to recruit and assemble the best team and give them the freedom (within reason) to do their jobs.

I say to all senior executive teams, '50% of your job is to recruit and retain – you should know how to recruit the best people and how to motivate and keep hold of them.' To be a good leader, it is essential to truly know your people, what makes them tick and how to drive them. A good leader should be available for discussions and have an awareness of people's home lives – always remember that there is life outside work.

This is just one part of the leadership equation though; you also have to manage the operation. This involves checking and challenging; holding people accountable; coaching and teaching people to grow and get better in their work. Another key skill is knowing how to motivate. A good leader should be able to motivate all individuals and teams so that they are constantly striving to achieve better results across the business. They should carry out suitable appraisals on a regular basis and discuss any training or development needs that would help each team member to further grow, and ensure no one becomes a blocker. They should create continuous improvement plans and include celebration as a key part of this, setting targets that can be achieved regularly and within a fairly short time period. These targets can be extended once the team becomes familiar with the process.

## The Three Cs

We run a workshop with new managers across our various businesses that teaches them the basics of how to be a good manager. This is particularly important and valuable if it is their first management position. In SMEs, most people tend to not get any formal management training and so create their own style based on their experience. If you've ever had a really awful boss and a really great one, you will likely deploy more of the style of the good than the bad, because you've experienced it for yourself and it's how you'd want to be treated.

On these management courses we teach many things, one of which is how to performance manage people most effectively. For me, it boils down to three simple things, which I call the Three Cs:

1. Clarity
2. Competence
3. Consequence

People need clarity on what exactly is expected of them. Your competence as a manager is shown through the training, coaching and mentoring you provide on how to do something. The consequence can be good or bad. If your team delivers what is expected of them, what does that look like? If they don't, what does that mean?

The best managers and leaders that I have worked with genuinely care about their people. They want to help them become better and progress in their careers. I sometimes say that being a manager is as much about knowing about what's going on in your employees' personal lives as it is about keeping on top of their work performance. List your top ten staff and write down their partners' names, their favourite food, their hobbies, their kids' names. If you don't know some or all of these things, you need to get to know your staff better and understand them on a deeper level.

## Tiny noticeable things

There is a brilliant motivational speaker whom I have had the privilege of hearing several times, named Adrian Webster. Adrian wrote *Polar Bear Pirates*, a work of fiction about a group of polar bears living on an iceberg.[5] The iceberg is melting and the younger polar bears realise they need to change because one day the iceberg will have completely melted. The older polar bears don't want to move as they like where they live. The book uses different characters to talk about leadership, management and how to drive

---

5  A Webster, *Polar Bear Pirates* (Bantam, 2003)

change in a positive way. Change should be constant. If you don't or can't change, you won't be able to adapt to market forces and new competition or innovation.

Adrian also tells the story of a salesperson who had travelled the world during an extensive career and had worked often with another salesperson, who'd also travelled the world selling her own products. After thirty years, the second salesperson was retiring. As a leaving gift, the other bought her an expensive bottle of champagne. You might think this was a nice touch, but having travelled around the world together he had never noticed that she was tee-total. Adrian talks about Tiny Noticeable Things;[6] these are little bombs of joy that you can set off that motivate staff, such as a handwritten 'thank you' card posted to the staff member's home address when they've gone above and beyond. Or a birthday card. Or knowing that their kids are in a school play and giving them time off so that they can attend. Or, if you know that someone enjoys red wine, giving them a bottle to say thank you for being awesome.

It's important to have fun with your team. This is often overlooked, but an effective team is one that works hard but enjoys that work. This attitude should be transmitted and facilitated throughout the business, as people who enjoy what they do usually put more effort into it and so deliver stronger results. As part of this, you should celebrate success on a regular basis.

---

6  A Webster, *Tiny Noticeable Things* (Wiley, 2021)

This does not have to be costly – a tray of doughnuts on a Friday afternoon can work wonders.

## Make meetings productive and essential

You learn something new every day. Every deal I do, every situation I face, whether in business or my personal life, has the potential for a new experience. These new experiences are immensely valuable as they offer opportunities for learning. Then you can think, if you are faced with the same situation again, what would you do differently?

My good friend, and COO of Opulentia Capital, Mathew Wainwright introduced me to a book by Gino Wickman called *Traction*.[7] It's a great read, in particular the chapter about meetings. Meetings can be boring and seem a waste of time. I adopt Wickman's model in my business, so meetings only happen when they are essential. We have an executive team on-site meeting once a quarter where we spend half the time looking at the numbers and performance of the business and half-solving two or three problems or challenges. In smaller team meetings, we spend more of the time discussing how to solve problems.

If you pulled up your work calendar right now, how many meetings are scheduled over the next week?

---

7   G Wickman, *Traction: Get a grip on your business* (BenBella Books, 2012)

Most calendars are overloaded with meeting invites and, more often than not, employees leave thinking it was a waste of time.

But meetings can be a great use of time. When run effectively, meetings foster collaboration and communication, keeping employees motivated. A staff meeting, for example, can cover critical topics that affect the entire department or company. But if it's not well organised, collaboration and communication may be undermined and the meeting will be unproductive, with attendees wondering whether it was necessary.

To increase productivity and overall morale, consider why some meetings feel like a waste of time. Is it because they either have too much of something (they happen too often or they're too long), or not enough of something (focus or actionable outcomes)? There are some things you can do to immediately improve and start running effective meetings:

- **Cancel unnecessary meetings.** Millions of meetings take place each working day (estimates range up to 56 million per day in the US)[8] but how many are truly necessary? While complex topics and creative discussions are best suited to in-person or video meetings, if you're simply sharing information, consider another more

---
8   E Short, SiliconRepublic (20 October 2017) www.siliconrepublic.com/advice/stress-work-meetings

efficient method. Written status reports or online check-ins work just fine in many cases and allow you to avoid too many meetings.

- **Establish a 'no meetings' day.** When your meeting reminder pings every hour on the hour, it's tough to find the focus to dive into your next project. You want to give the important work you're doing the time and mental space it deserves, but meetings seem to be dominating your day, even when you're not actually in them. Schedules riddled with meetings interrupt deep work and that focused time you need to tackle complex issues and important projects. Even once you get better at cancelling unnecessary meetings, regular interruptions that prevent you from focusing have a negative impact on your overall output. Owning your time is critical to boosting your productivity. Try spearheading an initiative that keeps your team's calendars meeting-free on, say, Thursdays, or any other weekday. Make it part of the culture.

- **Reject meeting invitations.** Every meeting invite has the option to decline, but how often do you click that box? Look at the agenda, the attendees and the duration. Empower yourself and your team to be selective about what you commit your time to at work and click 'decline' if you don't see the benefit. If needed, block out parts of your calendar to show people that your head's down working and that you'll decline invites during that time. You can always ask for the minutes afterwards so you can follow up if need be. Chances are, though, you'll be just fine.

## Time management

Your time is a valuable commodity. The average meeting length is 50.6 minutes,[9] but that doesn't mean every meeting has to be that long. More often than not, meetings can be cut in half if you just get a little creative.

When you plan your meeting agenda, estimate how much time you'll need for each topic, add up the total time and then set the appropriate meeting length. Maybe all you need is fifteen minutes, or maybe you need forty-five. Whatever the case may be, participants will be more focused when they know they've got ten minutes for a particular topic. A sense of immediacy will keep the discussion on task and ensure all agenda items are covered so you don't have to schedule another meeting for the items you failed to get to.

In the tech world there is a thing called a 'stand-up'. This is a quick daily status meeting where team members remain standing as they report on what they've just done, what they're doing next, and what problems they see ahead. If you have a recurring status

---

9   'Productivity Trends Report: 1:1 meetings', Reclaimai (2 November, 2021), https://reclaim.ai/blog/productivity-report-one-on-one-meetings

meeting, try a fifteen minute stand-up with your team rather than booking a conference room for a thirty to sixty minutes. You don't have to stand together huddled near your desks. You can meet over coffee in the morning, outside on a nice day, or in a lobby area. The key is to pick something different from the norm of 'another meeting' so that people stay engaged, and to have a time limit. You can use a timer initially while you get used to the idea of the shorter timeframe. Hold people to it, too – depending on the size of the group, you may want to give everyone thirty seconds to a minute of speaking time each, then stop them and move on so that people get used to giving succinct and to-the-point status updates.

Whichever style of meeting you opt for, staying focused when everyone wants to talk about their weekend plans can be difficult, especially if your team is widely distributed or remote, as it can be a fun time to catch up with people you don't see often. Planning ahead and setting clear expectations for your meeting might actually get everyone enjoying their weekend earlier, rather than just talking about it. To keep things focused, there are various things you can do.

## Set an agenda

It's important to identify the purpose and goal of any meeting, so be sure to set an agenda that clearly states what needs to be accomplished – do this in advance and share it, rather than creating one on the fly. Having a concrete agenda in place before the meeting provides clarity to attendees and keeps everyone on track. Keep the agenda in a central place, like a work management tool, to easily tie agenda items to tasks and project timelines. Assign time blocks so you don't spend too much time on any one thing. If you want to include a little time for team bonding you can kick off a meeting with five minutes of unstructured chit chat, but be sure to stay on top of the time so you can move onto the important topics.

When you've got the agenda, make sure you send it alongside the meeting invite. Often, when you start creating an agenda before you set up the meeting, you find that you don't need to meet in person at all. If not, setting and sending an agenda with the invite gives people the option to decline if the content isn't relevant to their priorities. If you use a work management tool to create your agenda, you can add attendees as collaborators and allow them to view, add or comment on items before the meeting. This means everyone comes prepared and ready to discuss the topics of concern. There are plenty of handy templates out there that enable you to easily build an agenda for all kinds of meetings.

### Selective invites

For a meeting to be productive, everyone in attendance should have a reason to be there and a clear role. While inviting everyone you can think of to your meetings may seem helpful, it will actually make them less productive. Instead, ensure that only the right people are in the room, and that everyone knows their role and why they were invited. If half the agenda applies to only three out of fifteen attendees, you should rethink your agenda and/or invite list. This is another important reason to create an agenda before you schedule the meeting – once you've sent out the calendar invite, if a key person can't make it, reschedule rather than trying to meet without them, as you'll likely have to schedule a follow-up anyway.

One of the roles you should assign – in advance of the meeting – is note-taker. When one person is in charge of taking notes or minutes, the rest of the group can focus on participating rather than creating their own record. Notes are also helpful for anyone who might have missed the meeting. Make sure notes are shared immediately after the meeting and that all attendees can access them. Again, a work management tool is a great place to file meeting notes and agendas and enables you to keep everything in the same place.

## Chair

One particular kind of meeting that happens regularly and is of great importance is the board meeting. Running these well requires a dedicated role, that of chair. There are several terms that are frequently used to describe this role, including chairperson, chairman/chairwoman or chair.

However it's referred to, the role of the chair is incredibly important. While they don't need to be an integral part of the day-to-day business, the chair should understand enough about the business to ensure that any decisions made or ambitions set are relevant and achievable. This will stop short of detail, in most areas, but a headline understanding should ensure the chair knows what is realistic and sensible. It will also keep conversations with board members, or the senior team, relevant.

Dr Stuart Smith is a business veteran, having been CEO/chair of dozens of companies around the world. I've hired him as chair in some of the companies I've been involved in and he has assembled a winning team of experts in their field. I discussed with Stuart what being an effective chair involves.

The main tasks of the chair go far beyond organising and leading board meetings, as you'll see below. Their key functions and responsibilities are:

- **Build the board.** It is the role of the chair to ensure all board members are fit for purpose. They must be comfortable in their role and share the values and strategic plans of the company. They must pull their weight and be effective in their departments. They need to be good managers and leaders and know how to properly delegate so that their own teams are equally as effective and successful. If there are any skill gaps, there needs to be a plan to fill them, either internally or externally, for example through the appointment of one or more non-executive directors.

- **Focus on strategy.** The chair has a key role in putting in place a quality strategic plan for the business that looks three to five years into the future. The creation of such a plan is best achieved by involving as many of the team as is relevant. Most of the board would be included, along with many of the management team, but it is also common to involve other members of the team where they have interests or opinions that could be relevant.

- **Set high standards.** The chair should lead from the front in setting high standards of management, leadership and governance. They should apply best practice within the relevant industry sector and aim to be better than the competition. They should carry out benchmarking exercises to monitor performance and ensure it matches the best in the sector. Where there are specific technical, compliance, legal or customer standards in place, they should ensure that the systems in place are appropriate and will enable these to be achieved.

- **Provide support** to all members of the board and other senior managers, in particular the CEO or MD and the rest of the board. The chair should be available to hear and discuss issues and concerns.

The role of CEO or MD can sometimes be a lonely one, as they cannot always talk about issues they are experiencing with their team, especially when they are expected to know all the answers. These are conversations they can have with the chair, who should offer help without interfering.

- **Work with shareholders.** This will ensure that their needs and expectations are met in terms of specific goals and targets. The chair should provide a bridge between shareholders, the board, and the entire team, to promote harmony at all levels. Where shareholders are also directors, the chair should manage the different levels of responsibility and avoid any misunderstandings or potential conflicts between these. They should also provide suitable KPIs for shareholders so that they get regular performance information.

- **Represent.** The chair should represent the organisation in an appropriate way at all levels of the business and in the media. They should work with the board and senior team to connect with other interested parties including banks and other lenders, suppliers, customers, government agencies, auditors, accountants, insurers, health and safety bodies, acquisition targets and more. Assist others to join in with this representation to achieve widespread recognition as a professional and successful group of people.

- **Oversight.** The chair should provide a link between shareholders and directors to ensure that all requirements are adequately met. Where shareholders are remote, the chair sets up regular communication systems and relevant KPI reports to present them with performance figures that show that goals and targets are being met, or, where they are not, the plans that are in place to rectify the situation. The chair should also maintain high-level oversight of each department and how they are working to deliver the budget/plan.

- **Comply with regulation.** Not only will there be various legal, technical, company and other statutory regulations that need to be adhered to, but there can often be further strict rules and procedures in place, such as HR items, health and safety items and other specific targets unique to the business. The chair needs to be sure that systems are in place and that suitable people have been identified and made responsible and accountable for achieving agreed outcomes.

- **Comply with constitution.** The chair should be aware of any relevant shareholder agreements and the Articles of Association for the company and deliver all items that are covered in these documents. This will include ensuring suitable notices have been sent out ahead of any meeting, checking that enough board members will attend to cover any quorum issues, all rules relating to retirement and election of directors are fulfilled, and any need for a formal vote on significant matters is included in the agenda.

- **Lead discussion.** The chair should provide the catalyst for top-quality debate and always ensure that all members of the board get the opportunity to present their views. They should control any members who are impatient to get their opinions on the table to maintain a healthy debate and dampen any tendency to get over-excited and/or loud. People can get passionate in business and keen to express their views but should respect the need to hear different, even opposing, views.

- **Create subcommittees.** These may be needed to share out some larger responsibilities across multiple people. The chair may, but doesn't have to, be the chair of the subcommittees. Example subcommittees include those responsible for remuneration, health and safety, human resources, facilities, and so on. The membership of each subcommittee needs to be relevant but not too large – a maximum of six would be a good target, comprised of those with a genuine interest in the overall purpose of the subcommittee.

- **Manage meetings.** The chair should plan suitable dates, times and venues for board meetings, issue an agenda promptly and ensure that quality minutes are taken and distributed to all attendees. The chair should arrive early to welcome members (and any guests) and then maintain momentum, manage breaks and avoid any tendency to waste time, encouraging all attendees to participate.

The chair needs to be resolute, determined, persistent and fair. A number of other specific skills are required to be a good chair, and a few more are needed to become a *great* chair. Several of them are common to other senior management or leadership roles. Sometimes this understanding can be acquired on the job; in other cases, it may be useful for the chair to enrol on a relevant course. In brief, the key skills of a great chair are as follows:

- **Actively listen.** When you are actively listening, as opposed to passively listening, the person speaking receives your full focus and all other thoughts are put on hold. It often requires the listener to wait until a suitable break in the conversation arises before giving a carefully considered response.

- **Show genuine concern.** This is related to active listening. The chair should aim to ensure that all members of the team feel part of the group, are fully involved in the business, committed to their role and working towards their goals and targets. The most effective teams are those that work effectively and enjoy what they do. Promoting harmony within the team enables them to be and achieve more than just the sum of the various parts (or individuals).

- **Communication.** This is a key skill and must be a constant focus, as the chair is the bridge between shareholders and the board. Communication is in all directions, with all shareholders and board members; doing this effectively can take quite a lot of time. In the current era, some of this can be virtual, but the chair will need to have sufficient time available for in-person communication.

- **Include everyone**. The chair should take on board the opinions, thoughts and views of all members so that they can contribute to any final decision. They should try to involve those who are usually quiet and reserved but who are likely have useful contributions. Where it is beneficial to seek further advice or information from beyond the current group, then outsource and identify sources of excellence and expertise where it is needed.

- **Remain neutral.** This can be difficult, especially if the chair has strong views of their own but is essential when managing a team. The chair must seek and consider all views and work towards a consensus on a decision and/or plan. If the chair tries to force through their own views, they are no longer acting as chair but as a consultant or other expert. They should aim to influence without dominating.

## Summary

Having the ability to recruit great people, then getting to know those people and understand what makes them tick, giving them the tools and resources to develop and a platform on which to grow, are the keys to a successful business. This begins with leadership. Great leadership is a combination of things, not least of which is having the vision, foresight, and the charisma to get your people excited about coming to work.

Meetings are a necessity in most businesses, but they are not always essential. To get most engagement in and impact from meetings, only conduct them when absolutely necessary, only invite people who definitely need to be there and always create and distribute an agenda in advance.

One of the most important leaders in an organisation is the chairperson. The chair should be able to articulate the company vision, the strategic plan and any updates to it, and communicate it across the company and beyond. Only when the overarching vision of the business is deeply understood by the whole team will they be able to focus their activity on delivering it.

## THREE
# Reaching Customers

You can have the best salespeople and the best sales processes in the world, but without the right marketing strategy you are doomed. It never ceases to amaze me when I talk to business owners who 'don't really do marketing', don't have a strategy, rely on word of mouth and cannot list any USPs.

Some entrepreneurs think they have to invent something new to be a success, yet the vast majority of businesses are generally selling the same product or service as their competitors. It is rare for something entirely new to be invented. Look at James Dyson, the founder of Dyson. The product he was selling was a Hoover, which already existed, but he tried to make it different/better by not having a bag to empty. Whatever it is you are selling, think about *why* someone should buy it. Usually, the answer is because it's better or cheaper than a competitor, however, I would rarely enter a market purely to sell something cheaper as there will always be bigger players with deeper pockets who could crush you.

Why someone should buy your product or service is something you need to communicate through your marketing. Marketing is essentially getting the word out there about what your company does and/or sells and exactly what's so great about it, and keeping telling people.

Prior to acquiring my real estate business, the customer proposition was flat. Fundamentally, it was based on people, service and producing nice photographs of the customer's property (which weren't even that great). To improve the proposition, we extended our opening times (so buyers could connect with us outside of working hours), improved our marketing, advertised in more places and even produced our own property magazine that we distributed to buyers. We had a centralised call centre staffed with telesales agents who could better respond to enquiries and generate new business. These USPs gave customers more compelling reasons to do business with us rather than our competition.

## The Four Ps

After people, the most important aspect of a successful business is getting the marketing right – this is assuming you already have a product or service to sell that is big enough to scale. One of the first basic marketing theories I learned about was the 4Ps:

1. **Product:** The first thing to identify is the product (or service) you are selling. Is it a saleable product? Can you sell it for a profit? Is the market big enough?

2. **Price:** The price at which you sell your product or service has to enable you to make a profit but also reflect what your target market is prepared to pay.

3. **Place:** This is where you will sell your product, which could be a high street store, online, a mix of both, or some other channel.

4. **Promotion:** How will you promote your product to your target customers and how will you convince them to purchase it?

Let's look at the four Ps in a business that's easy to understand, let's say a car wash business. Your business model is that you get paid to wash cars for the general public.

Your **product** is pretty simple – time spent washing a car. You can also upsell extra products and levels of service (like vacuuming the car inside, adding air fresheners, tyre prep).

In terms of **price**, you could position yourself as the cheapest or the most expensive. Before setting your price, you need to work out your costs. Your fixed costs will be: staff wages, water, cleaning products. Four full-time staff plus materials might cost, let's say, around £15k a month. You then need to find the point of equilibrium that generates enough volume but makes a profit. If you charged £10 per car wash, you would need to clean 1,500 cars a month (or 50 a day if you were open seven days a week) to break even, which seems reasonable.

The **place** where you operate your business will have a big impact. If you choose an out-of-town location, you would have to put up posters and hand out flyers and advertise to ensure people found you, which will increase your costs. Or you could choose a main road location with passing trade, where your **promotion** costs will be less. In the right location, you essentially have free advertising. On the other hand, you could try to win corporate contracts and offer to clean a company's vehicle fleet – think bus depots, transport companies etc.

## Market research

You'll see from the above example that in order to make effective use of the four Ps method and make the right decisions on produce, price, place and promotion, it helps to know a bit about the market you'll be operating in and the customers you're hoping to attract.

Market research is the process of gathering information about your target market and customers to identify their needs, predict the success of a new product, help your team iterate or innovate an existing product, and understand brand perception to ensure your team is effectively communicating your company's value. Market research allows you to meet your buyer where they are. As our world (both digital and analogue) becomes louder and demands more and more of our attention, this insight is invaluable. By understanding your buyer's problems, pain points and desired solutions, you can craft your product or service to naturally appeal to them.

Many companies fail to do market research, or don't undertake it properly or thoroughly enough. When I first started my recruitment business, I researched my competitors and found what would make my company better (headhunting). In the companies we acquire now, we carry out detailed market research to create a marketing plan that will be crucial to the future growth of the company. Think of it as an experiment. You can hypothesise about what the outcome of the experiment will be, and you won't know until you actually try it, but you can canvass opinion from experts and potential customers. When we acquire a business and we take a walk around the shop floor, the factory, or the office, we quickly get a feel for what the business is like and how it positions itself in the market. Having a robust marketing plan based on market research is crucial and updating and adapting this as the market changes should be an ongoing task of the business.

Market research can answer various questions about the state of an industry, but it's not a crystal ball that marketers can rely on for insights on their customers. Market researchers investigate several areas of the market and it can take weeks or even months to paint an accurate picture of the business landscape. Nevertheless, researching just one of those areas can make you more attuned to who your buyers are and how to deliver value that no other business is offering them. Certainly you can make sound judgement calls based on your experience in and knowledge of the industry and your existing customers.

Keep in mind that your competitors also have experienced individuals in the industry and an existing customer base. It's possible that your immediate resources are equal to those of your competition. Seeking a larger sample size for answers can provide a better edge. Remember that your customers don't represent the attitudes of an entire market; they represent the attitudes of the specific segment of the market that is already drawn to your brand.

Market research provides insight into a wide variety of things that impact your bottom line, including:

- Where your target audience and current customers conduct their product or service research

- Which of your competitors your target audience looks to for information, options, or purchases
- What's trending in your industry and in the eyes of your buyers
- Who makes up your market and what challenges they face
- What influences purchase decisions and conversions among your target customers
- Consumer attitudes about a particular topic, pain, product, or brand
- Whether there's demand for the business initiatives in which you're investing
- Unaddressed or under-served customer needs that can be turned into selling opportunities
- Attitudes about pricing for a particular product or service

Ultimately, extensive market research allows you to gather information from a large sample of your target audience, eliminating bias and assumptions so that you can get to the heart of consumer attitudes. As a result, you can make better business decisions from knowing the bigger picture. Market research can be either qualitative or quantitative in nature, depending on what kind of studies you conduct and what you're trying to learn about your industry or sector. Qualitative research is concerned with public opinion and explores how the market feels about the products currently available in that market. By contrast, quantitative research is concerned with data, and looks for relevant trends in information gathered from public records.

There are two main types of market research that you can conduct to collect actionable information on your business's products and/or services: primary research and secondary research. Let's dive into these.

## Primary research

Primary market research is the pursuit of first-hand information about your market and the customers within your market. It's useful when segmenting your market and establishing your buyer personas. Primary market research tends to fall into one of two buckets: exploratory and specific research.

Exploratory primary research is less concerned with measurable customer trends and more with potential pain points and customer challenges that would be worth trying to resolve. It normally takes place as a first step, before any more specific research is carried out, and may involve qualitative research techniques such as open-ended interviews and/or surveys with small numbers of people.

This exploratory market research is then often followed by specific primary market research that is used to dive deeper into the issues or opportunities that have been identified as important. In specific research, a smaller or more refined segment of the target audience can be identified and then canvassed for their views, with the aim of solving a particular identified or suspected problem.

## Secondary research

Secondary market research involves analysing all the data and public records you have at your disposal, to draw conclusions related to, for example, trends in your industry. This data might include market statistics, industry content and existing sales data for your business. Secondary research is particularly useful for analysing your competitors. The main sources your secondary market research can draw on are:

- **Public sources:** These are your first and most accessible source of material for conducting secondary market research, and are often free to access.

- **Commercial sources:** These often come in the form of market reports, consisting of industry insight compiled by a research agency. You will typically have to pay to download or access these insights.

- **Internal sources:** These deserve more credit for supporting market research than they generally get. This is the market data your organisation already has – average revenue per sale, customer retention rates and other historical data on the health of old and new accounts – all of which can help you draw conclusions about what your buyers might want right now.

## Raising your profile

Another indirect mentor and someone whom I have met and heard speak several times is Daniel Priestley. Daniel is an Australian-born entrepreneur who lives in London. He runs an amazing business called Dent Global and has written bestselling books on marketing and business.[10] One of the strategies he talks about is positioning yourself as a Key Person of Influence in your industry. If you want to make it big in a particular industry, you need to present yourself as an expert. If you are just starting out, then a way to do this is to create a joint venture with someone who is well known in your sector – maybe they sell to the same customer base or industry as you, but have a different product. You can then leverage their influence in return for a percentage of sales, for example. Meanwhile, you can work on building your profile by writing articles, blogs, perhaps even a book.

When Daniel Priestley explained the Key Person of Influence concept, he emphasised that at the centre of every industry there is an inner circle comprised of the most well-known and highly valued people in

---

10   https://danielpriestley.com

that industry, the 'Key People of Influence'. It is likely that you are already aware of these people in your own industry because their names tend to crop up in conversation, for all the right reasons. They attract a lot of, and the right type of, opportunities. They earn more money than most, without a struggle. These are the people who bring success to the projects in which they are involved – and everyone knows it. Given their connections and the regard in which they are held, Key People of Influence enjoy a special status in their chosen field, so they tend to be invited to join the best teams and projects and can often set their own terms. They are given VIP treatment, treated with respect, and others listen when they speak. Unsurprisingly, these people are in demand – all this means that they don't chase opportunities, they curate them.

If you're thinking it must take years, decades even, to become a Key Person of Influence, you're wrong. Nor do Key People of Influence need degrees or doctorates, or opportunities and wealth inherited from a well-positioned family. While time invested, qualifications, talents and a wealthy family might be helpful, they are not a reliable way to make yourself a Key Person of Influence. At the same time, there are plenty of people who have been active in their industry for years and yet are not Key People of Influence. There are many MBAs and PhDs who are not yet Key People of Influence. There are people with immense talent and/or privilege who aren't Key People of Influence either.

Daniel's own story is the perfect example of this. He arrived in the UK in 2006 with little more than a suitcase and a credit card. He knew no one and didn't have a big budget to start a business. Yet within a year, he had gained a reputation as one of the best-connected entrepreneurs in London. With his partners, he built a business turning over millions – now, high-flyers and heavy-hitters in his industry are just a phone call away. Given that London is known for being a difficult place to break into established networks, initially Daniel was told it would take years to be accepted in the right circles. Not so. London is like any other city in the world in that it is full of people, and people everywhere respond to the ideas he talks about. Daniel's advice is: if you are not one already, it's not difficult to become a Key Person of Influence within your industry, even within the next twelve months.

## Social media

I do not profess to be an expert on social media but, for a business, it is a powerful tool for marketing. Social media can reach millions of people, of which many will be potential customers. Used correctly, you can target those potential customers, to meet them where they are and post the content that will appeal to them and their interests. You can use Facebook ads, for example, to target a certain demographic or area, or Instagram to create powerful and far-reaching video content. The type of content you use here is key

– people don't want to see a TV advert, but you can utilise influencers connected with your target market to promote your product in an educational way. For example, let's say you are selling jewellery, you could pay an influencer to showcase your jewellery in their Instagram story. Twitter, on the other hand, is a great platform for engaging with customers or getting them talking about your product.

## Becoming oversubscribed

The ultimate aim, or endgame, of marketing – the ideal state to arrive at – is to have a business with more customers than it needs. In a conversation I had with Daniel Priestley, he explained how to become oversubscribed and create endless demand for your products or services.[11]

People are willing to queue to get into certain restaurants. There are some products you need to pre-order months in advance. Tickets for certain tours sell out on the day they are released. Some stocks shoot up in value as soon as they are floated. Cars are bought before they've been built and properties sell when they are nothing more than a set of drawings. Some consultants are booked six months in advance; some hair stylists can charge ten times more than others and still have a waiting list. There are bottles of wine that are purchased while their grapes are still hanging on

---

11  Interview with Daniel Priestley, September 2018

the vine. What all of these people and businesses have in common is that they don't chase clients, clients chase them.

Why does this happen? We live in a world of endless choices. Why do people line up, pay more, and book so far in advance when other options are more readily and cheaply available? Why are some people and products in such high demand? This is a phenomenon known as being 'oversubscribed'. A product or brand reaches a level of being oversubscribed when there are far more buyers than sellers; when demand massively outstrips supply; when many more people want something than capacity allows.

Daniel's company runs large business and leadership events around the world. They don't use typical conference rooms in typical hotels; rather, they host events in theatres and auditoriums normally used for musicals and shows. What's more, these events are premium priced and oversubscribed – despite the fact that many companies struggle to attract 50–100 people to a free business event. In January 2013, Daniel sent an email to clients in Sydney, Australia that said: 'We have sold too many tickets to the event that you've booked in for. The venue holds 700 people and we've now sold more than that and have a waiting list forming. If you'd like to sell your ticket back to us – or for any reason you can no longer attend the event – please email us, and we will buy back your ticket today for double what you paid for it.' Say one person bought a ticket for $100, to sell more tickets Daniel's company would buy back the ticket for $200 then resell it for, say, $500.

This event was brand new with a high-end price tag – and Daniel's company didn't have a single staff member on the ground in Sydney at the time. The email wasn't a joke, a gimmick or a ploy. It was genuine. Too many tickets had been sold. A similar problem occurred in Melbourne two weeks later, then in London, then in Florida. This wasn't happening by accident. It was orchestrated.

In Daniel's business, clients are often booked three months in advance. This isn't done to be difficult; it's just the amount of time people need if they want to work with his company. If someone isn't sure, there's no argument or hard sell. They don't need to convince people to work with them – there are others lined up waiting.

One of the ways he keeps himself oversubscribed today is through the process of sharing big ideas. The more he shares, he has discovered, the more people want. He also believes that the principles he espouses lead to better businesses for everyone involved: the customers get a higher level of service, the business owners stop chasing and the employees enjoy working for a company that's in demand.[12]

---

12 D Priestly, *Oversubscribed: How to get people lining up to do business with you* (Capstone, 2020)

But first, he says, before you even begin, you must be confident that your offering is something that genuinely serves people. You must be passionate about it and the value it represents to the world. You must not only love what you do, but care about your customers and want to be in your business for the long haul. Being oversubscribed is a way for you to do your best work and spend more time with your current clients rather than chasing new ones. This approach gives you more downtime to innovate your products rather than running around selling them. It allows you to build your brand rather than blend in with the crowd.

## Sales

The best salesperson in a successful business is the business owner. They are the most passionate about what they do and so will always be the best person to sell their product or service. But if they want to scale the business, the business owner needs to rely on a sales team to do the selling. A lot of organisations have various policies and procedures in place, but rarely do I see sales processes properly documented. If you work in finance, there is probably a documented policy on how to raise a purchase order, or how to get expenses authorised. In my experience, in sales it tends to be a case of a new salesperson turning up and being told to 'go out and sell'.

If you do not have a sales process, get one written and make sure it includes the following:

- What should happen from the point that a lead comes in from your marketing?
- Who should talk to the customer?
- When?
- What should they say?
- What objectives will they have?
- What documents, eg a fact-find, should the salesperson have as prompts?
- What printed materials or presentations are needed?
- How does a salesperson close?

Once you have documented processes for all of these areas, they should form the basis of your training programme for all your salespeople.

You may have heard the saying, 'Turnover is vanity, profit is sanity but cash is king'. You already know that 95% of business start-ups fail in the first five years – but this is not necessarily because they are not profitable, more often it's because they run out of cash.[13] For example, I looked at acquiring a training business

---

13   M Houston, Forbes (22 December 2020), www.forbes.com/sites/melissahouston/2020/12/22/how-this-cash-collector-turns-outdated-accounts-into-cash-quickly/?sh=738b0596d7a3

that had £5m turnover, £1m of which was profit, but was on the verge of going bankrupt. How can a business with £1m profit go bust? It had run out of cash.

This business was a particularly interesting one – they were training foreign armies on how to diffuse bombs. They had ex-army and bomb disposal people who would fly into foreign countries and deliver this highly specialised training, which they did to the tune of £5m in global sales. I remember turning up to meet their MD and senior team at their UK headquarters and it was like a paintballing assault course. There were unexploded bombs (well, dud ones) and old army tanks. It was pretty cool. What wasn't cool, though, was their lack of cash. We needed to come up with a plan to turn the situation around, and quickly.

What had happened was that they had won a fairly lucrative contract with a foreign government for £800,000. They had delivered the training, but they hadn't been paid. They had incurred the costs of delivering the training (travel and accommodation for their team – not cheap). They had sent in their bill but 180 days later still had not been paid. It seems barmy that they didn't get some form of upfront payment to cover their fixed costs, but all their MD saw was an £800k sale. There was little thought for whether and when they would get paid.

This is an example of how a business can be profitable on paper, but can incur high costs before cash comes in – if it ever does. It doesn't take a rocket scientist (or should I say a bomb disposal expert) to work out that this is not sustainable. We didn't end up doing that deal, but we would have negotiated hard and chased the debt and/or looked at leveraging the rest of the debtors to plug the cash gap until the bad debt came in.

## The Five Cs

Growing a company organically is difficult, but the Five Cs can be applied to any business to significantly improve sales. For one of my businesses, this approach doubled the revenue per customer. We have just had a quick lesson on the importance of cash. The other four all lead, in different ways, to cash; they are:

- Crowd
- Conversion
- Cost
- Continuity
- Cash

Put simply:

$$Cash = Crowd \times Conversion \times Cost \times Continuity$$

In most businesses, by increasing each of the first four by just 5% you will generate circa 20–40% more cash.

Let's look at each of these in detail:

- **Crowd:** The crowd of potential customers is your target audience, your marketplace. This is probably the most difficult one to influence. I said earlier it is hard to organically grow a business. To increase the crowd, you must get better at putting your product/service in front of your target market – through increased or enhanced marketing, for example. Or, by educating potential customers who don't know that they need your product or service. To increase your crowd often requires better or more marketing spend, but if it's successful your cash will increase.

- **Conversion:** How many of your crowd do you convert into paying customers? This can be quite easily improved by refining your sales process – when a customer lands on your website, is it easy for them to buy your product? How can you make it easier? Think about Amazon – you can buy things with a couple of clicks. It could be training your sales team on how to better close. If you can increase your conversion, cash will go up.

- **Cost:** This is the cost of your product or service. You may think that business today is incredibly competitive and price sensitive, making it impossible to increase your prices. But think about all the products and services you sell – it would be much more difficult to increase the price of your main seller, but what about the things you don't sell as many of, could you increase those prices? Have you ever been on holiday to the Spanish Costas? There are some tourist resorts that have rows upon rows of bars with crazy offers like one euro for a pint of beer. They draw in crowds looking for the 'bargain beer' but then ramp up the prices of other items such as cocktails or food, where they make their money. This works across different industries. I once owned an automotive business. The pricing of automotives is pretty much set in stone, but not the service plans. It's easier to increase the prices of these supplementary products than the main event. If you increase your costs to customers, your cash will increase.

- **Continuity:** This is the number of times your customer returns to buy from you again. If you can increase this, clearly your cash will go up.

Let's look at a real-life example. I was involved in a real estate company where the business model was to sell residential properties and receive a fee for each completed sale. The problem was this was the *only* way the company made money. When we acquired the business, it was completing around twenty sales a month and charging customers an average of £1,500 per sale, making its monthly revenue £30,000. It cost £30,000 to run the business (in staff wages, premises, marketing etc) so it was just breaking even. All it would take was one bad month for the company to run out of cash.

The first thing we looked at was how we could better market the business to reach more of the crowd. We revamped the website and looked at other advertising. This was before social media had really taken off, so to reach more target customers involved leaflet dropping, direct mail and newspaper advertising.

To improve conversion, we hired great salespeople and trained the existing team to convert better, teaching them how to close and overcome objections. We also gave the customer proposition an overhaul and offered potential customers more compelling reasons to use us. We designed a more rigorous sales process that included more detailed fact-finding so we could prioritise more motivated customers. For example, if one potential customer was just 'thinking of moving' and another was selling their home to relocate for work, the latter was prioritised in the sales pipeline.

All the above led to a much more premium offering that enabled us to double our fees, charging a premium price for a premium service. When we acquired the business, the company was only making money from completing property sales. We introduced a number of other services that benefited the customer and generated revenue, which meant customers bought from us more often, improving our continuity. When buying and selling property, most people need a mortgage and a conveyancing lawyer to handle the transaction. Property investors may need the services of a rental agent. You get the gist. Rather than start offering all of these additional services ourselves, we created joint ventures and earned commissions by referring customers who went on to buy products and services. On average, per customer we made:

- Property sale – £3,000

- Conveyancing sale – £250

- Mortgage arrangement fee – £1,000

- Rental referrals – £250

- Auction referrals – £500

This is what the business looked like before and after:

|  | Before | After |
|---|---|---|
| Crowd | 7,000 | 9,000 |
| Conversion | 3.3% | 5.0% |
| Cost | £1,500 | £3,400* |
| Continuity | 1 | 1.12** |
| Cash | £346,500 | £1,713,600 |

* Our average property sale fee was £3,000 but, with the addition of the other services that were upsold, our average revenue per customer was £3,400.

** On average, 25% of our customers bought conveyancing and 33% bought mortgage services.

Of course, dealing with this extra volume did increase our costs (mainly through marketing and staff resources) but this was gradual over three years, during which time our turnover increased from £346k to £1.7m.

## Crossword selling

A great way of illustrating to your team the power of upselling and cross-selling is what I call the crossword selling technique.[14]

To put this into practice, you need to create a board that has all your customers listed on the vertical axis and all your products/services on the horizontal axis. You then colour in the squares of the 'crossword' for every service or product the customer buys. Then you can work out what the uncoloured squares are worth. This is a powerful tool to get your staff to buy into as it enables you to make more money from what you have. It's easier to upsell to an existing customer that you already have a relationship with than it is to attract a new one.

I acquired a business in the leisure industry whose main product was caravans. We wanted to improve productivity within our workshops. One of our upsell

---

14   Crossword selling technique included with permission of Jeremy Harbour.

## REACHING CUSTOMERS

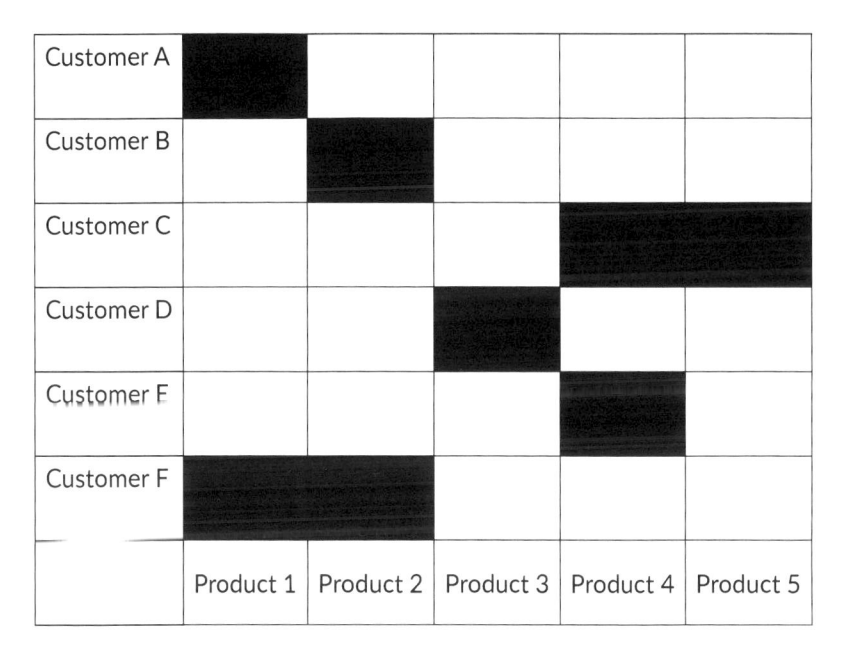

| Customer A | ■ | | | | |
|---|---|---|---|---|---|
| Customer B | | ■ | | | |
| Customer C | | | | ■ | |
| Customer D | | | ■ | | |
| Customer E | | | | ■ | |
| Customer F | ■ | | | | |
| | Product 1 | Product 2 | Product 3 | Product 4 | Product 5 |

*Crossword selling technique*

products was a motor mover. Some twin-axle caravans are pretty heavy to move on their own; a motor mover is a piece of kit that you install and then control with a remote control to move the caravan easily.

We discovered that, on average, our contractually employed staff could fit two motor movers a day. During busier times we would hire contractor engineers to take on the excess; they could fit four a day. We looked into this and uncovered a variety of reasons why external workers could fit double what our employed staff were doing. To address this, we implemented a bonus scheme for staff who improved their productivity. It worked a treat.

83

## Sales methodologies

When it comes to actively selling, there are various different selling methodologies that you can use, and some will be better suited to particular products, services and circumstances. Let's look at a few different strategies:

### Transactional selling

Transactional selling is a short-term strategy that focuses on making quick sales, where neither the buyer nor the seller has any interest in building a longer term relationship. This kind of sales method is scorned in today's relationship-focused era, but transactional selling still has a place in both B2B and B2C marketing communities. A good example would be cinema or concert tickets. Here, the business is selling low-cost, generic products and turns a profit by selling in large quantities. B2B companies also engage in transactional selling, for example by selling SaaS (Software as a Service) applications to small business teams. The only goal here is to provide a quick, frictionless experience to the customers.

### Solution selling

With solution selling, the sales staff try to paint a picture in the prospect's mind about what they currently lack and how their product can help them. Since the advent of the internet, this kind of sales method has fallen out of favour, since B2B buyers can easily find the solution to their problems themselves, without the need for a sales executive. For solution selling to be effective, the sales staff must have a good relationship with their customers, be able to anticipate their needs and sell not only the product but also the experience of purchasing it.

## Provocative selling

This kind of sales strategy tries to uncover customer pain points and unmet needs, typically through market research and customer surveys. It includes thorough data analysis and crafting a strategy that compels buyers to check out the product. Provocative selling creates a sense of urgency and drives sales by suggesting crises and threats on the horizon.

This approach is profitable, but hard to pull off. You need good expertise to pull the right triggers and manage supply and demand. The strategy can fail if customers do not feel the sense of urgency you are relying on.

## Collaborative selling

Focused on building long-term customer relationships, collaborative selling is more of a strategic alliance than a one-to-one sales process. To make this work, all your customer-facing teams, including both marketing and customer service teams, should be working towards the same goal of helping the customer solve their problem. If this is done right, the sales team can become a long-term partner for the buyer and continue to suggest solutions to improve the business into the future.

### Inbound selling

This is the most powerful method of selling in the internet era. Since consumers today have more information about the product and possible solutions, some markers prefer to make customers come to them. In this approach, the marketing team creates personalised content addressing the specific needs of the customer, drawing them in to become part of the sales process. To succeed here, your content should be so interesting and insightful that customers trust your authority on the subject in question. Building this trust early on makes the job of the sales reps easier further down the line.

## Sales process design

As I have already mentioned, an effective sales process boosts conversions, ensures your prospects are highly engaged and provides all your customers with a consistent experience throughout the journey. When you are too focused on selling and scaling your revenue, it's easy to overlook the need to commit to the time-consuming process of building a highly effective sales process.

Your sales process is the series of steps your sales team takes to move a prospect from the awareness stage to a closed customer. A strong, standardised sales process helps your sales reps close more deals by giving them a clear and proven framework to follow; this will help them avoid mistakes that could cost the business customers. It also means that any new member of staff can quickly get up to speed and learn what to do and say at different stages.

Your sales process directly affects your revenue streams, so it's essential that you have a good one. If you follow the below steps, you will build an efficient sales process that allows you to continuously close leads.

## 1. Analyse your current sales strategy

Consider what's working and what isn't in your current sales strategy. This will help you tailor a process that works for your business. Sales affects your bottom line and you should take the advice of all stakeholders in crafting the strategy. Observe your sales staff in action and analyse the most recent deals and sales closed. What are the common points? What are the usual touchpoints? Consider how long the entire process took and what objections the customer had. Once you have an idea of the general time frame and touchpoints, you can pinpoint where inefficiencies and sticking points arise and find solutions to eliminate them.

## 2. Create a compelling buyer's journey

This is the most important step and one which many organisations miss. Creating a buyer's journey forces you to look at the process from a customer's perspective. You need to understand the common interactions they have with your sales reps, the problems they typically face and the solutions they expect your business to provide. The buyer's journey can be split into stages, each stage designed to solve particular customer problems and inspire a specific action. Dividing your customer journey helps you identify areas that need work.

A benefit of segmenting the buyer process is that you can define and design content that moves the prospect on through the sales process. Customers will move forward only when it aligns with their needs. Thus, each stage will address different pain points. Addressing these pain points will result in there being a pre-existing trust when it's time to actually purchase the solution. Work with your sales reps operating at different stages of the process and identify the common concerns shared by customers in each stage, then create content and solutions to overcome these.

## 3. Define a good lead qualification process

Once you set up your sales funnel, you are bound to attract leads that do not fall into your target audience radius. Your sales team must be able to identify such leads and eliminate them. This helps them focus on prospects that are highly likely to convert. You need to analyse the unqualified prospects and eliminate the content or platform that brings them in.

## 4. Measure your sales efforts

The sales process should be kept flexible, as your team will find new methods and work more efficiently, but you need to create a process that enables you to analyse sales efforts at every step so that you can optimise throughout the process. You need to ensure your team is co-ordinated and your marketing efforts are reaching the right target audience. Define KPIs that capture the performance of your sales strategy. These may include: number of leads generated, percentage of leads converted, churn rate at each buyer stage, revenue generated. The targets you set for these will depend on your sales and marketing objectives.

Mapping out a detailed sales process will give your sales team a clear and effective framework to follow that will help you to consistently close more leads and boost your revenue. A good sales process helps you provide a consistent experience to all your prospects, increasing your brand's value in the market.

Remember, every business is unique, so create systems tailored to your business.

## Evaluating your sales process

Creating an effective strategy is challenging and your work is never complete. Once you have a sales process in place, you need to continually review it and track its effectiveness. You'll need to tweak it according to the feedback you receive from customers and the impact you see on your bottom line.

### Sales cycle length

This is one of the most important parameters to look at. If your leads are moving through the sales funnel quickly, this means you have a content strategy that works and your sales reps are good at moving prospects along. Start tracking time the moment your prospects enter the funnel; knowing the average duration of the complete sales cycle will help you set targets and optimise the process.

### Close rates

By tracking the close rate, you can measure and manage the effectiveness of your sales pipeline. For example, if your sales closure rate drops from 15% to 10%, you can immediately see that there is a problem that needs to be fixed. Then you can analyse each stage and see where the customer churn is happening. If you make a change and see an improvement in the close rate, you can scale it to optimise the whole process.

### Pipeline churn rate

In a sales context, the 'churn' is how many prospects move through each stage of the funnel. If you are nurturing prospects slowly, your churn will be low; leads will accumulate and your pipeline will be full of stale opportunities, so you need to have a plan that nurtures leads in a timely fashion to keep them moving through. On the other hand, if your churn is high and you're running out of prospects, you have a lead generation problem. You'll need to adapt your sales process to scale your top-of-the-funnel activities and increase your prospecting. Ideally, you should have a pipeline filled with fresh, qualified prospects and no significant backlogs at any stage.

## Common sales mistakes

Unfortunately, mistakes in the implementation of the sales process are common. It is essential to define concrete, specific steps that your sales team can follow. Some of the main problems I see related to the sales process are:

- **Vague/ambiguous:** If your sales process is vague, it can be interpreted in different ways and your sales team (and so your sales) will be less consistent and more likely to make mistakes. Once you have created your sales process, document it – clearly outline each step and share this as a resource with your team.

- **Lack of flexibility:** Your sales process will never be perfect or complete and should always be a work in progress. You should be constantly measuring your success and checking in with your reps to uncover new trends or potential issues. Continually improving your sales process will help you have better, more relevant conversations with your customers and boost sales.

- **Misaligned sales and marketing:** Creating a sales process is futile if it's not aligned with your marketing efforts. The sales team needs content produced by the marketing team; marketing team needs feedback from the sales team to create content that speaks to customer needs. Sales and marketing teams are interdependent and must be reading from the same hymn sheet.

- **Too much focus on closing:** While sales is of course about closing deals, it's also about providing value first. Prospects come with a problem and your team must solve that problem before selling your solution. Personalisation is essential in today's world, but that's not possible if your only focus is on closing deals. Win the trust of your prospects and the closures will follow. Focus your strategy on providing value.

- **Irrelevant KPIs:** Measuring the wrong KPIs is an easy way to miss problems with your sales process. Identify and measure the things that have the *most* impact on your sales pipeline. Remember, it's not always about headline numbers. You need to dig deeper into the data to find opportunities to improve your sales process, break these down by team and make them responsible for their own KPIs.

## Selling complex solutions

When I was developing my recruitment RPO model it was clear that the sales cycle was going to be longer than just winning an assignment to place a senior executive with one of my clients. Pitching a company to handle all or a large chunk of their recruitment was going to be a big deal and a complex sell.

When devising a sales strategy, I read a book called *The Ultimate Sales Machine* by Chet Holmes.[15] The lessons in it hit home and I thought I would adopt some of Chet's strategies to target new customers to pitch the RPO model to. Of course, we planned to sell this to our existing customer base, but we wanted to use

---

15  C Homes, *The Ultimate Sales Machine* (Portfolio, 2007)

it to expand our customer base, which required a new approach.

First, we wrote a list of the one hundred clients we most wanted to do business with. The list comprised companies operating in our sphere of expertise (real estate and financial services) that were large enough to have high-volume recruitment requirements, and had a strong enough brand and appeal as a prospective employer to be of interest to the types of people we could supply. We then researched the CEOs of these companies to get their contact details (email, phone, address).

We asked our main client at that time, to whom we were already delivering RPO successfully, to write us a testimonial. This wasn't just any testimonial; this was a testimonial from the CEO of a large and well-known real estate company saying how much money we had saved him in real terms and how much we had improved his recruitment process.

We then created a sales letter consisting of four paragraphs outlining the benefits of our services. It was not printed on corporate letterhead; it was a plain A4 sheet with the testimonial at the top in large print and a 'PS' underneath the signature saying that we would call at an allotted time to discuss the content of the letter and, if this wasn't convenient, to call or email us to schedule a better time.

REACHING CUSTOMERS

This powerful letter had a 16% response rate. Out of one hundred letters, sixteen got a response. Four CEOs spoke to us directly and took our call at the allotted time. A further three had their assistants arrange a more convenient time. Seven referred us to their HR team. Two responded to say that recruitment was not on the agenda during the financial crisis. Of the fourteen we managed to have a dialogue with, we met ten of them. We closed three long-term RPO contracts worth a serious amount of revenue.

All from one hundred letters.

Our letter generated such a good response rate (most direct mail tends to achieve a response rate of 0.1–2%) because:

- We marketed in a different form. At this time, most people were doing email marketing to these kinds of prospects; we sent a hand-addressed letter.

- The testimonial explicitly stated how much money we saved a well-known CEO in the same business and explained the specific benefits they gained.

- The letter didn't look like a mailer, it was plain and unbranded.

- We sent it to the CEO – the person at the top. While they may have batted it down to the HR

95

department in some cases, that still got us an introduction by the CEO to the decision maker.

- The PS was powerful, giving a specific time and date to follow up.

We still use this strategy today when selling complex products or services, or those with a high ticket value. Here is the letter:

> *<Name of CEO> of <Organisation> has saved over £350,000 in 2007 from his P&L by working with MF Group. He has also improved his time to hire with new recruits joining three weeks sooner than previously. Staff retention has also improved by 23%.*
>
> *Private & Confidential*
>
> *<Addressee>*
>
> *<Address>*
>
> *<Date>*
>
> *Dear <Name>*
>
> *RE: Reducing your cost of recruitment, improving the calibre of candidates you recruit, faster*
>
> *By working with us, XXXXX have significantly improved the calibre of people they recruit, recruiting them faster and at a lower overall cost.*
>
> *Our unique solution is exclusive to the real estate industry and is not offered by any other provider.*

*We would welcome the opportunity to see how much we could save XXXXX and make the other improvement mentioned in this letter.*

*We look forward to speaking to you.*

*Yours sincerely,*

*Paul Seabridge*

*CEO*

*<Telephone Number / Email Address>*

*PS – I will call you on Friday 3rd November at 8.45am to discuss the contents of this letter. If it is not convenient, please have your assistant contact me to schedule a more convenient time.*

## Negotiation

The word 'negotiation' brings to mind big, high-intensity moments, but actually we negotiate in most aspects of business as well as in our personal lives. 'Daddy, can I have an ice cream?' 'Yes, if you behave when we go to the park you can have one when we get back.' Negotiation can be as simple as asking for something and agreeing to do something in return.

Over the years, I've learned that negotiating only works if you have rapport, because rapport is a precursor of trust. Meeting in the middle is not always a desirable outcome, though there will be a degree of give and take, bartering and compromise. Sometimes, walking away from a negotiation is better than agreeing a bad deal.

Every day at Opulentia we negotiate multi-million-pound acquisitions. As a buyer, we never want to pay what the owner wants and we don't want to risk any money at closing; the seller will always want the best price and all the money. Neither will get exactly what they want; it's about finding a compromise that works for both sides.

We always start by thinking about what a deal must look like. This is not just financial. In fact, with most of the companies I have bought, while price was a factor, there have usually been more important things, such as what will happen with the staff, whether we will invest in the future, are we going to wreck the business…

Finally, rather than saying yes or no, use 'if' to request something in return and never commit until you get that something. =='If you do this for me, I can do this for you'==, or, ==' If I do this, what will you do for me?'== Sometimes the things you ask for, or that the owner (in the case of an acquisition deal) wants, may not cost you anything. For example, letting them keep their company car or private number plate.

Being a good negotiator is important, not only if you want to buy companies, but in business in general – whether you are negotiating with a supplier, a customer, or a staff member. It requires empathy and the ability to build rapport. You have to be able to be pragmatic and see things from all sides to negotiate 'good deals'.

## Summary

Having a clear, effective and documented sales process and ensuring that all staff are trained and retrained on it regularly, with an emphasis on cross-selling, will put your business in the strongest possible position. This will enable you to reach more customers – without whom you have no business.

You'll need to think carefully about what marketing methods and sales techniques you want to use. Many ideas that worked five years ago are no longer working. For example, you may have used direct mail to market yourself, whereas now social media is a much easier way to connect with your audience. Remember, your ultimate aim is to become oversubscribed. Everyone is under pressure to innovate and get results. The decade ahead will be both challenging and inspiring. The pace of change is increasing and the world of business and society won't look the same ten years from now. For many people, this will be a great wave of change that sweeps them out to sea, while others will surf and enjoy it.

All deals, whether it's closing a sale, landing a contract or buying/merging a company, will involve negotiation. To excel, you must know what's essential to you, what you're prepared to compromise on and what a 'good deal' looks like.

**FOUR**

# Finance And Accounting For Non-Accountants

While you don't have to be an accountant to be successful in business, if you are going to run a business you need to be able to get your head around the numbers and what they mean. You can – and should – hire experts to help if this isn't your strong point, but as the business owner you will never grow if you don't have at least some understanding of the numbers.

In the British TV programme Dragons' Den, aspiring entrepreneurs pitch their business for an equity investment from an investor (a Dragon). If you have ever seen it, you'll know how cringeworthy it is when an entrepreneur is quizzed on their numbers and they haven't got a clue. Many CEOs are not accountants, but they do understand financial data and how to use it to make better decisions in order to generate better performance. There are a few key financial metrics to get familiar with as a priority, which we'll work through in this chapter.

## P&L

First up is P&L, being the profit and loss statement, sometimes known as the income statement. This is a statement that summarises your revenue (sales), the direct costs you incur to deliver your product or service (cost of raw materials), and your operating expenditure, which is what it costs you to operate the business (eg wages, premises, insurance etc). When you subtract your direct costs from your revenue you get your gross profit. Gross profit is the profit you make from selling your product or service before your operating expenditure. If you then subtract your operating expenditure from your gross profit, this leaves your net profit.

If your costs are more than you make in sales (or income), your business will be running at a loss. If your costs are less than your income, you will make a profit.

>Income – Cost of Sales = Gross Profit

>Income – Cost of Sales – Operating Expenditure = Profit (or Loss)

*Example Profit & Loss statement*

| Sales | |
|---|---|
| Lemonade | 593,849.00 |
| Chips | 393,940.00 |
| **Total Sales** | **987,789.00** |

| Cost of Goods Sold | |
|---|---|
| Lemons | 104,938.00 |
| Sugar | 24,958.00 |
| Cups | 98,493.00 |
| Ice | 10,500.00 |
| Potatoes | 89,403.00 |
| **Total Cost of Goods Sold** | **328,292.00** |

| Operating Expenditure | |
|---|---|
| Staff Wages | 440,394.00 |
| Advertising | 66,000.00 |
| **Total Operating Expenditure** | **506,394.00** |

| **Net Income** | **153,103.00** |
|---|---|
| Gross Profit Margin | 33% |
| Net Profit Margin | 15% |

Your gross profit margin can be calculated by dividing your gross profit by your total revenue (income) and multiplying by 100 (to get the percentage). Your net profit margin can be worked out by dividing your net profit by your total revenue (income) and multiplying by 100.

What is a 'good' profit will differ from one industry and sector to another, but you can look up the financial data of your competitors (via public accounts posted on Companies House) you will get a feel for the range and can compare your business's performance.

## Balance sheet

A balance sheet is a statement showing your business's assets, liabilities and capital. It is called a balance sheet because the assets should balance (be the same as) the total liabilities and capital. Assets can be tangible in nature (tangible assets), for example a building, plant or machinery owned by your company. They can also be intangible, such as goodwill or any things you purchase or develop and capitalise (for example, intellectual property). 'Goodwill' is an accounting term for the price of an acquisition over and above the book value determined by the company balance sheet. These are all fixed assets. Current assets are the more liquid assets, usually defined as assets that can be turned into cash within one year. These include cash held in the company bank account, debtors (money owed by customers or others to the company) and stock.

Liabilities could be creditors (people the company owes money to, such as suppliers), taxes due (VAT sales tax, PAYE/payroll liabilities/corporate tax), bank loans and overdrafts. Current liabilities are liabilities due within one year; long-term liabilities are those liabilities due after one year – such as a mortgage or a long-term bank loan.

Capital and reserves are retained profits and shareholder capital that is invested in the company as equity (share capital).

Total Assets less Total Liabilities = Capital/Reserves

When a company's liabilities exceed its assets, it is insolvent. It is against company/insolvency law in many countries to trade when knowingly insolvent.

There are some quick tests you can run on a balance sheet to understand your company's solvency and liquidity status. The 'quick' test is to divide the current liabilities by the current assets. A ratio of one or more means the company has enough liquidity to meet its current liabilities; a ratio of less than one means it does not.

Another useful measure is number of debtor and creditor days, and stock days. This will tell you how long it takes the company to collect the monies it is owed by customers, how long it takes to pay its creditors and how long it takes to turn stock.

$$\text{Debtor days} = \frac{\text{Trade Debtors}}{\text{Total Revenue}} \times 365$$

$$\text{Creditor days} = \frac{\text{Trade Creditors}}{\text{Cost of Sales (or Operating Expenditure when no COGS)}} \times 365$$

$$\text{Stock days} = \frac{\text{Average Inventory (stock)}}{\text{Cost of Sales}} \times 365$$

You can play with debtor, creditor and stock days to improve cashflow through a bit of financial re-engineering:

- **Debtor days:** If you were paid four days sooner than you are currently, how much extra cash would you have? To get paid sooner, you can deploy better credit control mechanisms such as issuing customer statements, sending reminders, chasers, phoning the customer.

- **Creditor days:** If you paid your creditors four days later than you do currently, how much extra cash would you have?

- **Stock days:** Stock is basically tied up cash, so the sooner you sell it and receive payment for it, the better. To sell stock quicker look at your sales processes and incentivise key personnel to remove obstacles to getting stock out.

In one business I acquired, by improving debtor days by three days, extending creditor days by three days and improving stock days by six, we generated over $600,000 in extra cashflow.

## Cashflow statement

Probably the most important statement of all, the cashflow statement shows how much cash the company has coming in and what cash it has going out. Unlike the P&L statement, this shows specifically when cash comes in and where it's coming from, for example customers or other sources (like investment, bank loans etc), and when cash goes out to pay expenses, taxes, dividends etc.

A few definitions that will help you understand your cashflow statement, balance sheet and P&L:

- **EBIT** is earnings before interest and tax.

- **EBITDA** (earnings before interest, tax, depreciation and amortisation). This helps determine the cashflow in a business that is free to service debt. When acquiring businesses, we tend to value it based on a multiple of EBIT or EBITDA.

- **Interest** is interest payable on debt like a bank loan, for example.

- **Tax** is any corporate taxes the company has to pay from its cashflow.

- **Depreciation** is where you account for the declining value of an asset. Let's say you have a transport business. Your business model is transporting goods for customers and charging a fee for doing so. To deliver you need trucks. There are high costs involved in buying a truck, but because they do a lot of mileage and take a fair bit of wear and tear, over time the truck is worth less and less. You can offset the depreciation in its value against tax. While this is a paper transaction only (you don't actually pay the depreciation charge), it is a real cost to the business because what you charge in depreciation you potentially accrue in capital expenditure when you come to replace the truck in three or five years' time.

- **Amortisation** is the same concept as depreciation but relates to intangible assets, such as goodwill.

When I took over my mum's nursery, the first thing I did was change the legal structure by putting a limited liability company in place. This made the business better structured from a legal point of view, as the liability was limited to the investment of the shareholders. I soon got a grip of cashflow once I discovered that parents of children attending were billed half termly (there are six terms a year in the UK education system) and not everyone paid when they were supposed to. This created a cashflow problem – the business was profitable but didn't always have the cash to pay the bills. I automated the invoicing process and put good credit control mechanisms in place, which quickly saw the business generating more cash than it needed. Cashflow problem solved.

*Example balance sheet*

| Current Assets | |
|---|---|
| Cash | 598,693.00 |
| Accounts Receivables | 593,894.00 |
| Inventory | 249,384.00 |
| **Total Current Assets** | **1,441,971.00** |

| Non Current Assets | |
|---|---|
| Plant and Machinery | 159,837.00 |
| Business Premises | 359,040.00 |
| Vehicles | 240,593.00 |
| **Total Non-Current Assets** | **759,470.00** |
| **Total Assets** | **2,201,441.00** |

| Current Liabilities | |
|---|---|
| Accounts Payable | 586,940.00 |
| Bank Overdraft | 50,000.00 |
| Credit Card | 10,000.00 |
| Tax Liability | 165,948.00 |
| **Total Current Liabilities** | **812,888.00** |

| Non-Current Liabilities | |
|---|---|
| Long Term Business Loan | 250,000.00 |
| **Total Non-Current Liabilities** | **250,000.00** |
| **Total Liabilities** | **1,062,888.00** |
| **Net Assets** | **1,138,553.00** |
| Represented by | |
| Share Capital | 1,000.00 |
| Profit & Loss Account | 594,859.00 |
| Reserves | 542,694.00 |

*Example cashflow statement*

| | |
|---|---|
| Cashflows from Operating Activities | 314,405 |
| Cashflows from Investing Activities | 60,594 |
| Cashflows from Financing Activities | 100,000 |
| **Net Increase (Decrease) in Cash** | 474,999 |
| Cash at Beginning of Year | 200,000 |
| Cash at End of Year | 674,999 |

## Economics: the basics

Underpinning all of economics is the concept of scarcity, which is one reason why economics is sometimes referred to as the dismal science. Humans are constantly making choices that are based on a cost–benefit analysis. On a market level, the impact of millions of people making choices based on perceived or actual scarcity and the related incentives to act creates the market forces known as supply and demand.

While having a basic understanding of economic theory isn't perceived as being as important as balancing a household budget or learning how to drive a car, economic forces impact our entire lives. At the most basic level, economics can explain how and why we make the purchasing choices we do. The four key economic concepts — scarcity, supply and demand, costs and benefits, and incentives — can explain many of the decisions that humans make.

## Scarcity

Everyone understands the concept of scarcity, whether they are aware of it or not, because everyone has experienced its effects. Scarcity refers to the basic economic problem that the world has limited (or scarce) resources to meet seemingly unlimited wants and needs. This reality forces people to make decisions about how to allocate limited resources in the most efficient way possible so that as many of their highest priority needs as possible are met.

For example, only so much wheat is grown every year. Some people want bread and some would prefer beer. Only so much of a given good can be made because of the scarcity of wheat. How do we decide how much flour should be made for bread and how much wheat should be used for beer? One way to solve this problem is a market system driven by supply and demand.

## Supply and demand

Sticking with the example of beer, if many people want to buy beer, the demand for beer is considered high. As a result, you can charge more for beer and make more money, on average, by using wheat to make beer than by using wheat to make flour. Typically, this leads to a situation where more people start making beer and, after a few production cycles, there is a lot of beer on the market (the supply of beer has increased) and so the price of beer drops. Although this is an extreme and overly simplified example, on a basic level, the concept of supply and demand helps to explain why last year's most popular product is half the price the following year.

## Costs and benefits

The concept of costs and benefits is related to the theory of rational choice and rational expectations that underpins the whole of economics. When economists say that people behave rationally, they mean that when people make decisions they try to maximise the ratio of benefits to costs. If demand for beer is high, breweries will hire more employees to make more beer, but only if the price of beer and the amount of beer they are selling justify the additional costs of the staff and materials needed to brew more beer. Similarly, the consumer will buy the best beer they can afford to, but not, perhaps, the best-tasting beer in the store. The concept of costs and benefits is applicable to other decisions that are not related to financial transactions.

University students perform cost–benefit analyses by choosing to focus on certain courses that they deem to be more important for their success. This might means cutting the time they spend studying for courses that they see as less beneficial. Although economics assumes that people are generally rational, many of the decisions that humans make are emotional and do not maximise our benefit. For example, advertising preys on the tendency of humans to act non-rationally with many advertisements aiming to activate the emotional centres of our brain and fool us into overestimating the benefits of a given item.

## Incentives

If you are a parent, a boss, a teacher, or anyone with the responsibility of oversight, you've probably been in the situation of offering a reward (an incentive) in order to increase the likelihood of a particular behaviour or outcome. Economic incentives explain how the operation of a supply and demand system encourages producers to supply the goods that consumers want, and consumers to conserve scarce resources. When consumer demand for goods increases, so too does the market price of those goods, and producers have an incentive to produce more of those goods because they can command a higher price. Alternatively, prices can rise when the increasing scarcity of raw materials or inputs for a given good drives costs up and causes producers to cut back and supply to drop; consumers then have an incentive to limit their consumption of that good and reserve it for their most highly valued uses.

In the example of a brewery, the owner wants to increase production so they decide to offer an incentive – a bonus – to the shift team that produces the most bottles of beer in a day. The brewery has two sizes of bottle, a 500 millilitre bottle and a 1 litre bottle. Within a couple of days, they see production shoot up from 10,000 to 15,000 bottles per day. The problem is that the incentive they provided focused on the wrong thing, the number of bottles rather than the volume of beer. They begin receiving calls from suppliers wondering when orders of the 1-litre bottles are going to arrive. By offering a bonus for the number of bottles produced, the owner made it beneficial for the competing shifts to gain an advantage by only producing the smaller bottles.

When incentives are correctly aligned with organisational goals, the benefits can be exceptional. Such incentives might include profit sharing, performance bonuses and employee share/stock ownership. However, incentives can go awry if the criteria for determining when a target has been met falls out of alignment with the original goal. For example, poorly structured performance bonuses have driven some executives to take measures that improve the financial results of the company in the short-term, by just enough to get the bonus. In the long-term, these measures have then proven detrimental to the health of the company.

## Insolvency and restructuring

If you have ever faced insolvency, you'll know it can be harrowing. I have acquired several businesses over the years through administration (known as chapter 11 in the US), whereby an insolvency practitioner is appointed to sell the company as a 'going concern' (usually as an asset sale), which preserves the company and saves jobs. Various insolvency procedures can also be used to restructure a business. I have mentioned administration and, in the UK, there is something called a Company Voluntary Arrangement, which is an agreement (registered with the courts) with your creditors to repay them a percentage of what they are owed (which can be 100%) over a period of time. I have used insolvency to restructure companies in the UK and in Australia. While the next sections explain specifically the UK insolvency structure and options, it is fairly similar in other jurisdictions, though the process may be slightly different or be called something else.

## Creditors' Voluntary Liquidation

Creditors' Voluntary Liquidation (CVL) is a procedure instigated by the shareholders/directors of an insolvent company, to prevent the compulsory winding up of their business. It involves a process through which the assets of the insolvent company are sold and the proceeds distributed to the company's creditors. At the end of the liquidation process, the company is dissolved. The process is managed by a liquidator and is also referred to as 'winding up'. Usually, a company goes into CVL after its directors realise that the business is no longer viable and that, once it ceases to operate (if it hasn't already), it will not be able to pay its creditors in full.

## Members' Voluntary Liquidation

A Members' Voluntary Liquidation (MVL) is a procedure through which the value of the assets of a solvent company is realised and the proceeds distributed to the company's creditors and members. The key difference between a CVL and an MVL is that, although both are voluntary, MVL is a winding up of a solvent company, while CVL is the winding up of an insolvent company. After an MVL, the proceeds go to the shareholders, whereas a CVL sees the cash realised from the sale of any assets returned to creditors. An MVL can be used by directors to extract the value of a company that is no longer needed. Whatever the reason for undertaking an MVL, it is the directors seeking to close the company in the most tax-efficient manner possible.

## Administration

Administration is a procedure which allows for the reorganisation of a company or the sale of its assets to prevent creditors from taking action to enforce their claims against the company. During the administration process, an insolvency practitioner is appointed as the company's administrator. The administrator takes over control of the company's business and assets from the company's directors, in order to achieve one of three objectives:

1. To rescue the company

2. To achieve better results for creditors than if the company were wound up
3. To realise assets to make a better distribution to secure or preferential creditors

## Pre-pack administration

A pre-pack is an arrangement under which the sale of all or part of a company's business or assets is negotiated with a purchaser prior to the appointment of the administrator; the sale contract is then executed by the administrator immediately after their appointment. Pre-packs enable the sale of company assets to be undertaken quickly (reducing the likelihood of important contracts being lost), preserving the brand and value of the business and, ultimately, improving returns for creditors.

## Company Voluntary Arrangement

A Company Voluntary Arrangement (CVA) is a compromise or arrangement between the company and its creditors, which is implemented under the supervision of an insolvency practitioner to address the company's financial difficulties. A CVA can allow companies to:

- Settle debts by paying only a proportion of the amount that it owes to creditors.

- Come to some other arrangement with creditors over the payment of its debts.

### Insolvency

Insolvency – when an individual or company can no longer meet their financial obligations to lenders[16] – is used every day across the world to restructure companies to give them a chance of survival. It is not an area I like to get involved in anymore; I find turning around struggling companies to be time consuming and challenging, but it is certainly something that can set a business back on a successful trajectory. Insolvency can sort out a debt problem or remove parts of the operations that are not good, but you should always have a plan for how you will do things differently following insolvency because if you do the same things, you will get the same result.

## Summary

Every business should make cash generation a priority. This starts with an understanding of the numbers, which requires you to collect and analyse data and then create and implement rigorous processes to manage your finances and keep on top of cash generation. Cash generation (or EBITDA generation and growth)

---

16 A Tuovila, 'Insolvencies: Definition, how it works, and contributing factors', Investopedia (23 May 2022), www.investopedia.com/terms/i/insolvency.asp

is one of the most important KPIs we track in any business. Even the non-accountants who run departments and have P&L responsibility understand the actions they can take to generate more cash. For example, a sales manager will know to credit check customers to make sure they are creditworthy and negotiate payment terms to ensure prompt payment.

# FIVE
# Productivity And Change

Improving productivity can improve the profitability and cash generation of your business. For example, if you are a manufacturing business, making your product more quickly will have a positive effect on your business.

To improve productivity in an organisation you have to identify and analyse the obstacles and constraints. This could be staff requiring more training on how to work quicker. It could be automating parts of the process to speed it up. It could be acquiring better tools or resources. For example, I acquired a business that produced windows for commercial buildings. At the time, the machines that were making the windows produced eight per day. We invested in a new machine that could do thirty. This meant that, when we won a contract to supply 10,000 windows to a prison, we could deliver (and get paid) quicker.

One of many things that hinders the productivity of a company is improper utilisation of resources, such as money and manpower. Putting effort into something that will not yield anything in return is a waste of resources, whether that's materials or time. By analysing your workflow, you can easily identify any unnecessary subprocesses and/or wasted resources. Often, it is identifying the problem that is the big challenge in a company. Once you figure that out, finding a solution should be a walk in the park, whether that's re-allocating resources or eliminating a subprocess. A proper distribution of assets and resources will improve your business productivity; to figure out the right distribution, though, you need to conduct workflow analysis.

## Workflow analysis

All of us will have come across some type of workflow, often without noticing it. Whenever data changes hands from human to human or human to machine, it creates a workflow. When you are the owner of a company or manage a workforce, workflow analysis is essential and will help you run your business well.

This knowledge is crucial if you want to maintain steady production. This topic is too vast for a thorough discussion of every detail, so I will instead briefly explain the basics of workflow analysis and why it's important for your business. The contents of this section should be extremely helpful for any small to medium business.

To fully understand workflow analysis, first you have to understand the workflow. Workflow means the flow of work. It is a sequence of tasks in a company or organisation that take place one after the other. Workflow analysis involves breaking down and thoroughly examining performance throughout all tasks in the workflow to evaluate productivity, so that you can make necessary changes to optimise efficiency at every step and in the workflow overall.

Workflow analysis is a pretty simple process but can, to begin with, seem complicated. There's a lot that goes on, so in the following section I will briefly break down what's involved.

### Data collection and analysis

First, you have to collect some basic information about the workflow. Depending on the information you gather, you will decide how to analyse and optimise the workflow. This begins with asking basic questions like, what is the role of this workflow in production? Does it need to exist? How often is this workflow used?

Answering these types of questions will provide qualitative data about the workflow. How many changes of hands the workflow has and whether it involves parties from outside the company etc are important parameters that you should evaluate carefully. Determining the quality of the workflow is vital for further analysis.

After evaluating the quality of the workflow, you will need some quantitative data – some raw numbers. Each step in a workflow is called a subprocess. The goal is to limit time consumption to make every subprocess more efficient, so first you have to figure out how much time each subprocess consumes, the difference between the fastest and slowest subprocesses, and the frequency of each subprocess. These will all be numerical values, hence the name quantitative data. Once you have both qualitative and quantitative data, it's time to analyse it.

Quantitative data helps you to identify a problem; qualitative data helps you get to the root of the problem and work out how to solve it. For example, quantitative data might reveal that one of the subprocesses is taking too much time, but whether that subprocess is vital or could be removed to increase efficiency, cannot be determined without qualitative data. Analysing both types of data gives you a thorough overview of your workflow and helps you decide what changes are necessary.

## Implementing changes

After identifying all the problems with your workflow, major and minor, you can implement changes for better performance. This is not a 'one-and-done' process. It's a bit more trial and error process, where you change something, keep a close eye on the data to see how the subprocesses and the overall workflow are affected, and then make further changes as necessary. If the desired outcomes start to become apparent, then the changes you've made become permanent and you should notify all relevant parties of this in the workflow of the changes.

Now that you understand how workflow analysis works, it should be clear what benefits it can bring to your business in regard to productivity, but to summarise:

- **Increased efficiency:** Good workflow analysis can boost the work efficiency of your company. Through workflow analysis, you get to see individual processes and the entire workflow from start to finish. You can decide which steps you should eliminate, or which would perform better if you established automated systems, for example, thus increasing overall efficiency.
- **Time savings:** In a production line, time is money. In fact, in any workplace, good utilisation of time is key to high productivity. The quantitative data you collect can enable you to scrutinise the

time consumption of each workflow and every subprocess within it. If you feel it's necessary, you can reduce the time allocated to a subprocess or remove it altogether.

- **Improved relationship with employees:** Workflow analysis involves close interaction between you and your employees. When collecting qualitative information about subprocesses and their feasibility, you exchange a lot of information. People open up to each other in these kinds of interactions. Due to busy schedules, there is little time to talk to your subordinates. Workflow analysis opens that gate. You can accumulate lots of different information besides what's necessary for the analysis, which helps the office environment and so is ultimately good for business.

## Unfreeze, change and refreeze

The change model I use, and which is widely used by organisations around the globe, was created in the 1940s by physicist and social psychologist Kurt Lewin, whose background in physics inspired his ice block metaphor for social change. The name of the model comes from the idea that an ice block can't be forced into a new shape without breaking. Instead, to achieve a transformation from one shape to another, it must first be melted (unfreeze), poured into a new mould (change) and then frozen again in the new shape (refreeze).

The aim of the change model is to understand why change occurs, implement the necessary changes and normalise them in the organisation's day-to-day operations. The ultimate goal is to change the status quo with minimal effect on processes or employees, while ensuring maximum ROI. By considering change as a process with three distinct stages, organisations can better prepare for a new status quo. They can minimise potential complexities along the way and design a plan to manage the transition. Following this model also helps organisations adjust to the change and achieve stability while minimising chaos and discomfort for employees and other stakeholders.

The first stage, unfreezing, primarily aims to create awareness about the upcoming change. In the change stage, the actual implementation happens to support the transition. In the final stage, refreeze, the goal is to achieve stability and equilibrium after the change. Companies can apply the change model to change multiple processes or conditions, such as:

- Existing systems, structures or processes
- Behaviours, attitudes or skills of the workforce
- Corporate culture, to enable people to work together and collectively pursue the organisation's objectives

Change is inevitable for companies of every size and in every industry. Yet many organisations struggle to adapt. Often, there are misunderstandings and chaos before they can adjust to the change. Resistance to change is another common problem, even if the potential benefits of the change are known or apparent.

The unfreeze, change, refreeze model is an attempt to manage change based on an understanding of the change process, creating a plan for a smooth transition and overcoming any possible resistance in advance. The model helps create awareness of the upcoming change and the motivation behind it so that everyone affected by or involved in it is prepared and accepts what's coming. It also creates an environment where employees don't perceive change as a threat but a way to improve the organisation and contribute to its strategic vision. Below, I'll talk you through the three stages of Lewin's model in more detail.

### Unfreeze

This first stage is usually triggered by a motivating event that demonstrates a need for a change to occur, such as falling profits, a lawsuit or employee dissatisfaction. Once the decision has been made that change is needed, a change management strategy has to be communicated throughout the organisation to prepare employees for that change.

The organisation must prepare by creating awareness about the upcoming change while identifying and addressing any potential resistance. Senior leadership and managers should explain to employees why the organisation can't continue with the current way of doing things. To support their message, they might refer to financial statements, talk about declining sales, or explain the problems caused by negative customer reviews. They should also try to address any strong feelings, denial, uncertainty or doubt among the workforce, explaining why the change is required and how the organisation will benefit.

Some of the key activities during the unfreeze stage include:

- Examining the existing structures and processes to determine what needs to change and why
- Communicating the logic and benefits of the upcoming change to all stakeholders
- Engaging with the relevant stakeholders to get their buy-in
- Framing the motivation for the change in terms of the organisation's vision and mission
- Addressing employee concerns and getting organisation-wide support for a new status quo

Detailed analyses of the current state of the organisation and effective communication about the 'why' of the change are vital during the unfreeze stage. Neglecting either of these may heighten existing resistance and make it more difficult to move on to change implementation.

## Change

After the proposed transformation is properly communicated, the next stage is to implement the change as quickly and as seamlessly as possible. In the change stage, the actual implementation of the change(s) to the company's organisational structure, business practices, staffing or other areas takes place. Changes may vary in type or degree, depending on the company's needs, but they should always be carefully considered with input from employees and other key stakeholders. Often, people know they must act in a way that aligns with the agreed company direction, but may struggle to adapt to the new reality. Consequently, it may take time to implement all required changes.

To minimise roadblocks, the preparation of the first stage is vital. Leaders should share all relevant information with the workforce to ease them into the transition and address any problems or challenges early. Leaders should also take time to explain how the change will benefit employees. A clear ongoing communication strategy and strong leadership skills are the main pillars of a successful change stage. During the transition, senior staff members should re-emphasise the nature and purpose of the change and ensure employees never feel disconnected from the company or the change effort.

It can be helpful to engage with influential stakeholders and get them to act as change evangelists. It's also important to celebrate small victories and visible results so that everyone feels involved in the change effort and works as a team to make it happen. Some of the other important activities that happen during this stage include:

- Clarification of any misunderstandings or rumours
- Clear explanation of the effect of a change
- Involvement of line managers to provide day-to-day direction

## Refreeze

The final stage is about solidifying the change, so that the modifications made in the second stage become normalised and internalised in the organisation's daily activities. This process is often slow because it can take a long time for employees to get used to new practices or procedures.

The refreeze stage is crucial for ensuring the changes last and that the workforce accepts the new status quo. It also prevents employees from returning to older, less-preferred methods that may be detrimental to the organisation. Organisations can adopt both informal and formal mechanisms to freeze and sustain the new changes. The goal is to eliminate any lingering doubt or resistance and ensure complete organisation-wide buy-in to the new normal.

Important activities during the refreeze stage include:

- Offering rewards to reinforce the new state
- Identifying and eliminating lingering barriers
- Setting up a feedback system to collect employee comments and address any new issues or concerns
- Modifying the organisational structure, culture and policies to align with the change and reinforce the new way of working
- Providing employee training and support to ensure employees are comfortable and to eliminate anxiety and doubts
- Establishing quantitative metrics to measure success and communicate progress
- Business transformation initiatives

## The House of Change

Change is emotional, even when it's for the better, and we all deal with it in different ways. In business, the most successful and profitable businesses must constantly change. If you want a different result – increased profits, a better experience for customers, more staff engagement – you need to do things differently, so if you want to increase your profits, you'll have to make changes.

'The House of Change' is a great exercise to run with a team to kick-start a change management process. I have developed a theory that I call the Four Rooms of Change. In the process of change, we go through different phases. I liken these to four rooms – the Contentment Room, the Denial Room, the Confusion Room and the Renewal Room. People can reach these rooms at different times, and we all move through at our own pace. There are a few doors off those rooms that we can also slip into if we encounter challenges.

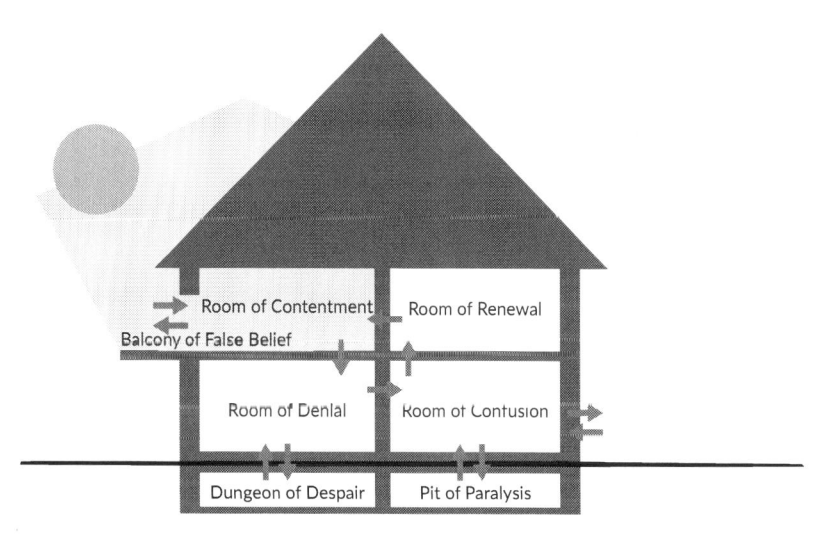

*The Four Rooms of Change exercise*

Let's take an example, where you work in banking. Google, Apple and Amazon have all entered the banking business. Their previous huge success means they have acquired a big cash position and they have begun to offer financial services including credit cards and commercial loans.

When we're in the Contentment Room of the House of Change, we don't see a need to change. Our current situation is satisfying and we have no desire to for anything to be different. In this case, we've been banking a certain way for years and it pays off. Why change? People can get stuck here for a long time.

Then Google makes their big move and we are caught off guard. We are triggered into the next phase and we enter the Denial Room. Yet we still don't see the threat. Why would we change? Google doesn't have our banking experience and our customers are familiar with our bank and our ways. People can get stuck in this phase and fall into the Dungeon of Denial.

But once the need for change is accepted, you enter the Confusion Room. Here, fear, anger and (internal) conflict take over. We don't know how to react because the situation is new to us. 'How can we compete with Google? Are they also entering the mortgage market? What are other banks doing? I should have seen this coming… they have such a big cash position.' It takes dedication and commitment to get to the next phase. The big risks in this phase are over-analysing the current situation and possible outcomes and getting stuck in the Paralysis Pit, or just plain giving up via the Wrong Direction Door.

When it all falls together, we enter the Renewal Room. We have made up our minds, worked out a new approach and are ready to take up the challenge. We know how to deal with the new threat, we have trained our clerks to respond to customer questions about Google. But the journey doesn't end here; we should prepare ourselves for another ride through the house – we don't know what's up next.

Share the theory with your team and use an example applicable for your situation. Other examples include:

- Print media vs the internet
- Book press industry vs the Amazon Kindle
- ICQ and MSN Messenger vs Facebook chat
- Telecoms industry vs Skype
- Nokia vs the smartphone with touch interface
- Classic mortgage loans vs public loans
- Fund investments vs direct investments by individuals

People in denial (of change) are often hard to deal with because they'll also deny that they're in denial. Deal with this by emphasising the need for change.

Provide facts. Repeat the 'why' of the change at every opportunity (at the coffee machine, in a meeting, with a presentation). Acknowledge, don't ignore, their feelings. Listen to what employees have to say. Talk to them, put everything on the table.

Involve people who resist. They may still use their energy to complain and push their feedback but try to use this energy to your advantage. Those who react apathetically or have given up will be more difficult to get on side than those who care.

## A one-page strategy

All change should be strategic, should move you closer to realising your vision for the company. Sharing this strategy can hugely help with getting team members on board with change. I mentioned earlier that a good leader is someone who can define a strategy and vision and get the team to buy into it. Here is an example of a strategy on one page devised by the executive team of a business I was involved in. You can see it gives a basic outline of the company's strategy: the who, the what, the how, the measures. It's essential to have measures so you can determine if and when the strategy has been delivered and you know what success looks like. It is all on one page so it is easy to refer to.

# Vision
To become the most respected agency in our field.

# Strategic Intent
To achieve £650k in profit by the end of 2020. We will do this by leveraging our expertise/offering and using this to develop digital and social media across multiple channels and sectors.

## 5 Strategic Pillars

| Grow our presence in the markets in which we play. (SLH/MAC) | Continue to sell the planning and proposition function. (RAM/AI) | Develop and grow the digital proposition. (RAM/JW) | Attract, develop and retain outstanding talent. (JA/SLH) | Identify and then grow at least one additional service or sector. (SLH) |
|---|---|---|---|---|
| **People** 1. High engagement and high performance 2. Coaching and feedback 3. Clear standards | **Customer** 1. Customer advocacy through excellent advice 2. Clear commercial outcomes 3. Excellent customer delivery | **Value** 1. Focus on sales pipeline to drive growth 2. Disciplined cost management 3. Don't be scared of price | **Licence to Trade** 1. Our No 1 client will never be our business 2. Sensible agreements and contracts in place to support key relationships 3. Clarity of offer/proposal for new deals | |

### KPIs
Gross profit. Net profit. Weighted pipeline.

## Brand Promises to Client. We will...

... always strive to find the most creative solutions for your issues and opportunities.

... always be on time, or budget, on brief – and keep you informed.

... challenge you, but always be on your side.

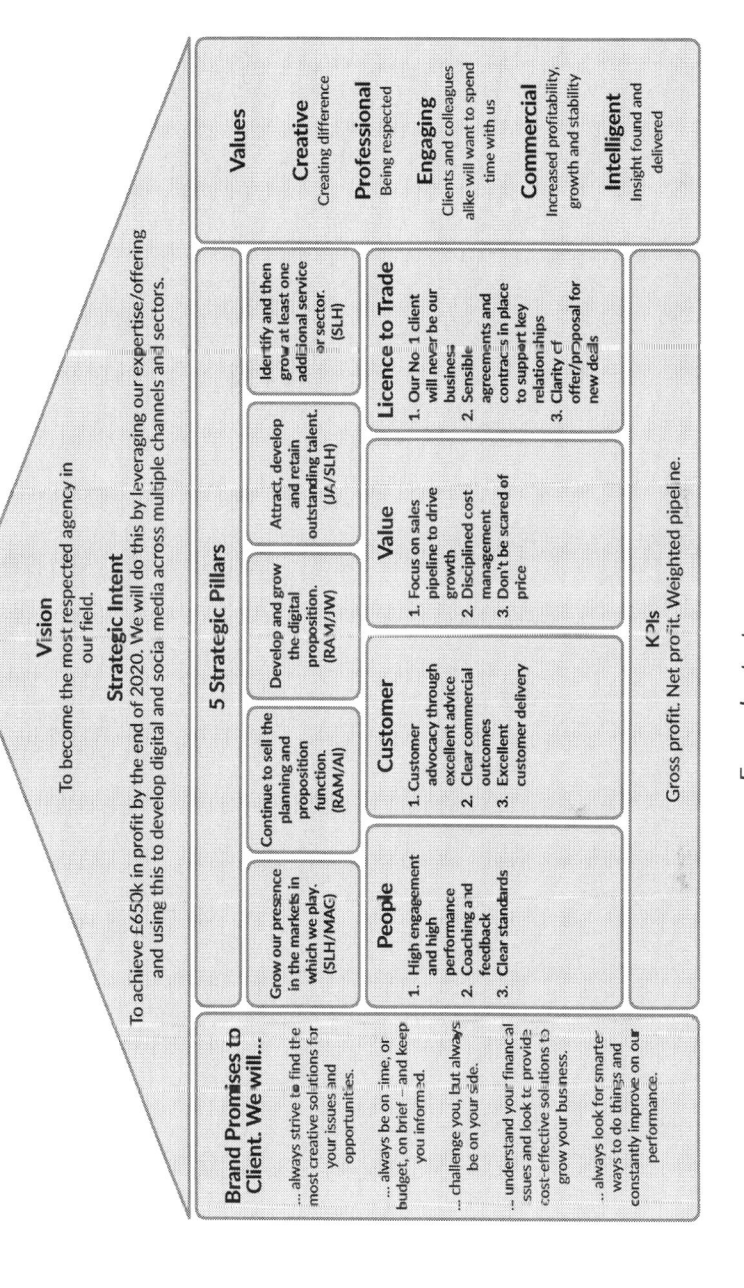

... understand your financial issues and look to provide cost-effective solutions to grow your business.

... always look for smarter ways to do things and constantly improve on our performance.

## Values

**Creative** — Creating difference

**Professional** — Being respected

**Engaging** — Clients and colleagues alike will want to spend time with us

**Commercial** — Increased profitability, growth and stability

**Intelligent** — Insight found and delivered

*Example strategy one pager*

## Summary

Any business owner striving for success should always have an eye on productivity; organisations are not static, consumers change, technology changes, the market and environment changes around them and what is efficient and effective one day, may not be next month. Productivity and profitability are inextricably linked, so monitoring is essential.

To improve productivity in an organisation you have to identify and analyse the obstacles and constraints. Workflow analysis is a relatively new idea but has proven valuable to business owners and entrepreneurs. If you think it can help you, I suggest you start work on it immediately. If your analysis reveals a need for change, be sure to involve your employees in the implementation. If they feel engaged in the process, they will be more likely to accept change, and be both more positive and more productive.

## SIX
# Mergers And Acquisitions

Mergers and acquisitions are the only sure fire way I know to double the size of your business in an afternoon. By selling companies you can create meaningful wealth that gives you choices in life, that allows you to go where you want, with whom you want, and do the things you want.

My paradigm shift came in 2015 when I decided to move away from running businesses. My time is now spent sourcing and doing deals (mergers, acquisitions, investments), which is where my expertise lies. My amazing team takes care of the operations and growth plans – they are much better at this than I ever have been or will be. This gives me the freedom to live and work where I want, and I don't see work as work. What's more fun than finding, negotiating and securing multimillion dollar deals from the gloriously sunny Mediterranean?

## Blowing the myth

The myth that you need lots of capital to do acquisitions is just that – a myth. I have completed over eighty transactions, most with no money down, or at least not my own. I invest my wealth in boring things that create passive income streams: real estate, commodities and structured investment products. I don't use or risk my own capital to acquire companies.

Think about when you buy a house, do you pay for it all in cash? No, most people borrow the money from a bank in the form of a mortgage. Buying companies is the same. Some of the largest deals are still done this way. In the UK, the Issa brothers acquired ASDA, a major UK supermarket, from its owners, Walmart in a £6.8bn deal made up mostly of debt.[17]

At Opulentia, we have devised a model to buy well-run, profitable, established companies in fragmented marketplaces. We then roll up in that industry (essentially a process of buying up smaller companies and creating one larger one); when you start putting companies together you can create economies of scale, buying power and faster growth.

---

17   Z Wood, 'Asda sold to billionaire Issa Brothers in £6.8bn deal', *Guardian* (2 October 2020), www.theguardian.com/business/2020/oct/02/asda-sold-to-billionaire-issa-brothers

In 2018, I met John Gardner. John is an ex-military man who, after coming out of the forces, spent two decades in the taxi trade. He was hugely successful building his own taxi business and then working for a private equity backed group to roll up in the taxi industry. I met John when he was helping a friend sell his taxi business. John had a vision to create the fastest growing taxi company in Britain and we joined forces. In under two years, the Take Me Group was formed and I helped John acquire seven companies. He has since built the group to almost twenty taxi companies with thousands of cars and drivers across the UK. When a taxi company joins Take Me Group they can instantly access economies of scale; they can tap into new technology, call centres and driver recruitment schools (to grow the business with more drivers).

Another industry I am involved in is the caravan and motorhome industry. In the UK this is hugely fragmented, with over 3,000 businesses. We have acquired five operators in this space to form a larger group, Falcon Recreation Group, which now boasts over £45m in turnover and makes substantial profits.

## Buy, build, restore

In all these deals, we utilised many of the tactics discussed in this book including cross-selling, improving margins and improving the environment for employees. We have perfected our model whereby, when we get into a new sector, we acquire a platform company: an all-singing, all-dancing business (well-established, consistent financials, good profits, capable management team) and we use that to roll up in the sector, either buying market share (buying competitors), related services/products (cross-selling, diversify income stream) or capability (buying up parts of the supply chain/improving margins). We then use the improvements to the business to drive synergies, using a model driven by my colleague Mathew Wainwright, Opulentia Capital's COO.

Our model of building a larger group inside a fragmented industry where there are lots of SMEs and few large enterprises is mainly focused on creating a win-win scenario for the different parties we work with, such as sellers, staff, banks, suppliers, customers, the shareholders and society. For sellers, we provide an opportunity to retire, move on to another venture or simply remotivate them while also meeting their financial needs. For us as a buyer, we will focus on running and trying to improve the company post-acquisition, while taking care of the brand, the reputation it has with clients and the staff. For the staff, we make sure that they are happy with our ownership, because if they are happy, they will make the customers happy. Our HR team takes a consultative approach towards how we, as the new owners, can make their life easier. Furthermore, as we buy more companies in the same industry, there is an opportunity for staff to move up the ranks if they show leadership potential, or relocate to other parts of the industry in which we have made acquisitions.

For the banks, the appetite to work as funding partners in different projects of the larger group also increases, because they have the security and backing of a larger company. The suppliers can now rely on a larger balance sheet and P&L, which typically represent security mechanisms that reassure them that they will be paid for the products they supply, as well as an increase in sales volume due to the upselling, cross-selling and down-selling capabilities that come from the larger group. The end customer is spoiled for choice and will want, or at least be exposed to, more of the services and products that are on offer. The end result of this group buildout is that all the parties involved end up in a more favourable condition.

## My biggest deal

When I met Mark Strachan in 2019, he shared his vision for creating a large food group. We agreed to partner up. Mark comes from a family of fruit farmers based in the Elgin Valley of the Western Cape in South Africa and he has started several small businesses within the food and beverage services arena.

Mark and I are in the process of building a £1bn food group, Aquila Food Group. The Aquila Food Group concept was born in early 2020 when Mark and I joined forces to embark upon an ambitious journey to roll up across several food and beverage verticals in order to create a first-choice major group in the food and beverage production and manufacturing sector. One that delivers a best-in-class wholesale experience for clients, constantly raising the bar in F&B standards and innovation, while achieving our goal in the most sustainable and socially responsible way to challenge the status quo. We surrounded ourselves (and will continue to) with industry experts who form a high-calibre team that share our vision and bring an abundance of passion and enthusiasm to the table to assist us on the journey.

The journey began in early 2021 when we acquired UK Salads Ltd, a £50m revenue company selling (grown and imported) fresh produce to UK supermarkets, in a leveraged buyout, as our first venture into this space. We have since gone on to acquire three other companies in just over a year and have almost £100m in revenue.

In attaining Aquila's vision, our first checkpoint will be to deliver a £1bn group turnover within five years, spanning seven food and beverage verticals (such as fresh produce, dairy and beverages). These verticals will house subsidiaries diversified across geographical areas, product complements and client concentrations, fuelled by an ambitious, multifaceted programme of acquiring the most synergistic subsidiaries through a highly targeted M&A approach, delicately integrating our new teams and companies to give our new colleagues autonomy and a platform for growth so that they can unlock their full potential, to the benefit of the group.

The food and beverage sector houses a highly fragmented SME market in which, through consolidation, we aim to achieve economies of scale, allowing us to report the consolidated group accounts to win larger, previously out-of-reach contracts, pool company resources and talent to drive synergies, and create the ground for a highly investable environment for ordinary capital market investors.

We explore opportunities within stable, well-run and profitable businesses with low debt that have an excellent reputation within their operating environment and have been in business for at least ten years but have either hit a growth and performance ceiling or their owners are looking towards retirement, or their next business venture. Our involvement takes the form of either an outright purchase ensuring the legacy of the founders continues, or a joint venture in a situation where the existing owners are still on a growth trajectory but are unsure how to structure the business going forward. Having founded and run businesses ourselves, Mark and I understand the intricacies involved, which allows us to navigate the best path ahead and become effective stewards of their businesses while we embark on a growth journey.

This ensures the longevity of the business as well as the team's well-being.

## The M&A process

There are deals everywhere. According to an article in *The Hill*, 40% of SME businesses in the UK, USA and Australia are owned by the baby boomer generation.[18] They don't have an exit strategy. Their kids don't want to buy it because they see how hard mum and pop worked; they are more interested in making money on YouTube. The businesses aren't big enough to be on the radar of private equity (who normally don't get out of bed for less than £100m). This creates opportunities for people like me who want to acquire, build and create a more valuable group. We do this by focusing on our people. We genuinely want to be the best place to work in that industry. Improving employee engagement is critical; we do this by investing in our people, giving them training, development and career progression opportunities as well as financial rewards for good performance and hard work.

Some of the best deals, though, are the ones you don't do. There are lots of companies out there that you can do deals on, whether it be a buyout or receiving a stake in return for some expertise. There are companies that

---

18  J Haar, 'Baby boomer owned small businesses can help resuscitate urban economies', The Hill (9 December 2020) https://thehill.com/opinion/finance/516132-baby-boomer-owned-small-business-can-help-resuscitate-urban-economies

## MERGERS AND ACQUISITIONS

are truly f***** and, while it can be tempting to 'do a deal', I've learned that there are some deals you just shouldn't do. I was recently looking at a marketing company, but discovered the owner had not paid any taxes (to the tune of a third of a million dollars), instead using the cash to overtrade, expanding the team and taking on larger premises. On paper the company had almost $1m in profits, but there was a huge hole in its finances.

In my time, I've bought three companies that, with hindsight, I shouldn't have. Now that we're not short of opportunities, we are not afraid to walk away if the business isn't one we know we can fix or add value to – or equally if the business owner is not someone we can work with. It's much better to do deals with people whose ethics and values you share and for companies you want to save. I am not discouraging people from doing distressed deals. There is a lot of money to be made in that space but it takes time, effort and a lot of patience. If you do enter this space, make sure you do your due diligence, you have a source for cash (as most need it), have a capable team to sort it out, and cover your arse, but don't be afraid to walk away. Sometimes, companies are too far gone and it doesn't matter how talented you are, you can't turn them around.

For the best chance of success, surround yourself with M&A experts who can help you navigate the process. Stay away from expensive lawyers, accountants, brokers. Instead, build your own team. Work with organisations like ours who help business owners and aspiring investors to acquire and expand their businesses through mergers and acquisitions. Once you've identified an opportunity for a deal and decide, after your due diligence, that you're going ahead with an acquisition, you'll need a legal agreement.

## Share Purchase Agreement (SPA) vs Asset Purchase Agreement (APA)

There are two ways a buyer can acquire a business, and two respective forms of legal agreement to facilitate a transaction. These are either by way of a share purchase or an asset purchase. (In the US, shares are known as stock, so a share purchase would be a stock purchase – stock should not be confused with inventory, in this context). In an asset purchase, the buyer acquires select assets and rights and sometimes assumes responsibility for certain liabilities relating to the target business. The benefits of an asset purchase are that the buyer can pick and choose which parts of a business to acquire and does not take on any legacy liabilities. By contrast, in a share purchase, the buyer acquires shares in the company (normally the entire issued share capital) from the company's shareholders. The buyer is purchasing the trading history of the business but assumes any liabilities as part of the transaction. Our preferred choice is to acquire shares via an SPA. In various jurisdictions, there are tax benefits for the seller of a business in a share purchase/sale.

## Share purchase agreement

The important clauses of an SPA include:

- **Sale and purchase:** This is the price and consideration, which may be subject to some form of adjustment mechanism by reference to, for example, 'initial payment' and 'deferred payment', where the total purchase price is divided into an upfront payment and further payment made after a certain time depending on various factors.

- **Conditions precedent:** Refers to any conditions that must be satisfied before the acquisition may complete. Failure to satisfy these conditions can give the damaged party the right to abandon the deal. An example of a condition might be certain consents from a third party.

- **Completion:** Details the timing and place of the acquisition, as well any actions required to complete (such as the date, whether it takes place at the principal place of business or with lawyers, paying the consideration) and what deliverables the parties are required to produce.

- **Completion deliverables:** These are documents that parties are required to deliver, such as stock transfer forms, board approvals and the statutory books of the target company.

- **Warranties:** A warranty is a guarantee, given to assure something is as promised and will remain so, and is typically accompanied by a promise of indemnification if this assertion proves to be false. With a breach of warranty, the party affected can claim damages to recover their losses.

- **Indemnities:** Indemnification clauses address liability for losses incurred due to misrepresentations and breach of warranties, covenants, and other agreements.

An SPA is substantial documentation and will usually be accompanied by several important ancillary documents, including a transfer of shares form, board approval, shareholders' approval and other due diligence documents.

### Asset Purchase Agreement

An Asset Purchase Agreement (APA) has the same substance and main clauses as a SPA, but with a special focus on the assets to be bought as opposed as to the shares. It is therefore key in an APA to include all the assets to be acquired in the schedule of this agreement with the necessary documentation. The due diligence also changes when proceeding with an asset purchase transaction because a formal document of ownership or key contracts will need to be provided. These documents can relate to the following types of assets: plant and machinery ownership, premises, stock or the benefit of business contracts.

## Legal structures

I always use a newly incorporated Special Purpose Vehicle (SPV) for any transaction. In group structures, I use separate limited liability companies to house different parts of a business for additional protection, such as an employee vehicle, asset vehicle, intellectual property vehicle. You can license IP for use (and monetise it) and keep liabilities and assets separate.

The Companies Act 2006 is the piece of legislation that serves as the main source for company law governing the UK. It covers almost every aspect of how a company should be run, managed and financed. The main aims of the Act are to simplify administration in relation to companies, protect the rights of shareholders and update and simplify corporate law.

In the UK, the main legal structures for a company are:

- **Private Limited Company:** A private limited company operates as a distinct legal entity to its directors and shareholders; the company is treated an individual in its own right. This means that all the business's assets, liabilities and profits belong to the company and the shareholders are not wholly responsible for debts incurred by the company. The company is owned by shareholders possessing private shares, but it is run by directors.

- **Public Limited Company:** A public limited company is also 'limited' in the sense that shareholders are not responsible for the debts incurred by the company in its capacity as a separate entity. The main difference from a private limited company is that a public limited company can offer shares to the public and, therefore, needs to be more open with information than a private company.

- **Limited Liability Protection:** This is a type of legal structure for an organisation where a corporate loss will not exceed the amount invested in a partnership or limited liability company (LLC). In other words, investors' and owners' private assets are not at risk if the company fails.

## Going global

I own companies around the world. My US-headquartered private equity firm, Opulentia Capital, has offices in several countries operating globally. I have found that many Western countries have similar opportunities and processes and laws, which means

MERGERS AND ACQUISITIONS

if I want to buy a company in Australia, which has different though similar company law and tax rules to the UK, I can.

My good friend and business partner, Aaron King, is an Australian citizen residing in Melbourne. He coordinates all deals on the ground and we complement him with our team and expertise based outside the country. We have also hired a corporate lawyer in Australia, who is a shareholder in our operations there. My first acquisition in Australia was a construction company in 2020 and I have since gone on to acquire another. Again, we used a leveraged buyout structure to fund the deal in the same way as I have explained with other examples.

I have a UK company that operates in Europe and North Africa. When we get into a new market, we hire experts that are familiar with the local rules. Similarly, whenever we are presented with a potential transaction in a country we have not worked in before, we hire an experienced local team, which will include a tax expert, legal expert and an operational team to run the business. We use the methods I explained earlier in the book to hire the best team.

## Raising capital

How do you go about raising millions of pounds (or dollars, euros etc) in funding for mergers and acquisitions? It may surprise you to discover that it's actually fairly straightforward. I won't provide an exhaustive list of all the different funding solutions, as there are many, I will summarise four deal structures that can be deployed. If you have never done an acquisition or don't own a business, it will be difficult to get the first one over the line so it may be helpful to partner with someone more experienced who can guide you through the process. But it is possible to do it alone. Before we get into the specific deal structures, I'll share with you some advice on raising investment from my good friend James Harbour, who helps business owners raise capital, whether equity or debt.

### Find a good match

You will, most likely, have thoughts whirring around about making sure an investor is the right match for your business. This is to be expected at the point where you're seeking investors. But potential investors are thinking the same thing. They need a business to be the right match for them and their investment portfolio. This makes things quite simple – go and find out what investments a particular investor has made before. Does your business sit logically alongside them?

Investors make decisions based on the information provided to them and that which they can obtain from the public domain. This means they will be drawn to strong business plans which contain a compelling narrative of the business. A great business plan will answer their questions and provide evidence of your intent and thought processes. It demonstrates that you've thought through the business, future growth and investment. No investor will part with their cash without a strong business plan, which should contain the following core information:

- Your target market with accompanying data
- Financial breakdowns and projections
- Sales and marketing channels with data to support your selection
- Marketing strategy and plans
- Competitor analysis
- Projected time scales and investment goals
- Potential problem areas and approaches/ solutions

## Be prepared

Investors expect you to be prepared, ready and able to be the business's greatest advocate. This means you're going to have to put in a lot of legwork before you even get to the pitching stage. Your request for investment needs to be clear, well explained and supported with evidence. It goes beyond passion – it's facts and figures that entice investment. You need to know and ask for exactly what you need, and have clear plans that anticipate how you will ensure a return on their investment. You need to clearly explain why you need the investment and where it will be spent. This requires a clear investment structure which details how investment can be legally made, including an exit strategy for the investor who, remember, ultimately wants a return on their money – they need to be able to see from the beginning where they will end up. All of this will be open to negotiation in due course, but you need to demonstrate that you have thought carefully about it.

### Business launch platforms

There are a number of different platforms where you can look for investors who might be a good match for your business. Some of the key ones are:

- **Websites:** There are many start-ups in need of investment, and so there are several websites you can turn to for help. They don't just help with investment but also the nuts and bolts of getting started. Two good examples are www.startups.com and www.gust.com.

- **Angel investors:** These are typically individuals with their own cash to invest alongside mentorship. Angel investors have created their own networks and platforms to collaborate and identify new investment opportunities. Top angel investor networks include: Funded.com, the Angel Investment Network (with regional branches), Angel.co and the UK Business Angels Association (UKBAA).

- **Social media:** Social media is a key place where investors look when hunting for new opportunities. A strong social media presence shows credibility. LinkedIn is particularly relevant here, enabling you to connect across industries and with investors.

- **Crowdfunding:** Crowdfunding sites are generally used as a way of getting support for a business idea from the general public, but angel investors in particular are no strangers to hunting down opportunities on these sites.

- **Private equity firms:** This is a traditional route for investors. They are mostly looking for large investments which will yield high returns, so are therefore best suited to businesses who anticipate significant growth in a short period of time.

- **Incubator and accelerator schemes:** By being part of an incubator or accelerator scheme, which provides intensive support and coaching to a cohort of start-ups over a set period of time, you can piggyback on the success of another business and benefit from resources.

## Structures used in acquisitions

You can acquire a company in a number of ways, each of which has different advantages and disadvantages,

Sometimes you will have a choice in which structure you use, sometimes the circumstances will decide this for you.

## 1. Leveraged buyout

To pursue a leveraged buyout, you need to first identify cash rich, profitable SMEs with meaty assets – look for unencumbered real estate, plant and machinery, trade debtors. You can leverage any of those assets to generate a down payment. Then you need to convince the seller to accept the rest of the purchase price in deferred payments – this is no different than paying off a bank loan in monthly instalments.

Having less debt and more profit on the balance sheet makes the company more viable. It is not about leveraging the f*** out of the company. We always do extensive financial modelling in any transaction to ensure it is affordable and not over-leveraged. Typically, we never commit more than 50% of the available cashflow in the business towards funding a deal. That means, in a company making $1m a year in EBITDA we would not use more than $500k in annual interest and debt servicing costs. In the event of a downturn in profits, this means that the profits would have to halve before we could not afford to meet our debt obligations. This is a pretty good hedge because we are buying well-run, long established, profitable companies with consistent profits. When we acquired Robinsons Caravans, we had a major supplier go bust and then a global pandemic that resulted in a lockdown. We still managed to service the debt because of this hedge and have since gone on to make record profits.

In leveraged buyouts, a lender and/or seller will always want security. But I do not advocate signing Personal Guarantees as this defeats the object of using an SPV (Special Purpose Vehicle), effectively a private limited company (with limited liability to its members). By signing a PG you break that 'limited' liability as you are underwriting what the SPV committed to – and if you sign a lot of PGs you increase your exposure. We generally have a security package that can include a limited cross-company guarantee. In larger groups, the parent company may offer a guarantee limited to the amount due at that particular time.

Debentures are an instrument available to business lenders in the UK, allowing them to secure loans against borrowers' assets. Put simply, a debenture is a document that grants lenders a charge over a borrower's assets, giving them a means of collecting debt if the borrower defaults. Lenders often take share charges as security for monies owing to them by a borrower under a loan agreement. A share charge will typically enable the lender to take control of the company in which shares are held upon enforcement.

In 2019 I acquired the UK's oldest caravan retail business, Robinsons, in a leveraged buyout. They sell over

1,000 new and used caravans (and now motorhomes) in the Midlands region of the UK. To acquire the business we leveraged the assets of the company (the company borrowed against its assets) to provide a cash payment to shareholders. In this case, the company owned the premises from which it traded, so we took out a mortgage against the property. It had significant cash reserves, which we enabled the shareholders to extract, and the rest was seller financed. We paid the balance in instalments.

## 2. Private placement

If you already own a business and want to expand by acquisition, private placement is an option. You can approach high-net-worth investors for a fixed term loan (or a bond), usually over five years, paying a coupon interest rate (giving them regular cashflow) and then they get their money back. You can deploy these funds into making acquisitions. This is a specialist area of corporate finance and when raising funds publicly there are rules to follow, so you will need a specialist team of professional advisers.

## 3. Going public

This may seem unthinkable. After all, a traditional IPO will take at least two years to complete and you need to have a decent business to take public in the first place. You can, however, create a SPAC (Special Purpose

Acquisition Company) and then, once listed, use the public stock (shares) as currency to do deals. A public listed company (PLC) will have greater borrowing power, allowing you to raise external debt including bonds, which can be used to fund acquisitions.

### 4. Shares as currency

Outside of acquisitions using debt, we sometimes do deals by offering our expertise in return for an equity stake in a company: sweat equity. In mergers, swapping shares for shares in a group can be an effective structure, giving you an opportunity to own a small percentage of something big instead of 100% of something small.

I purposefully haven't gone into lots of detail about any of these structures, each of which could be the subject of a book. If you want to know more about any of the structures and how to do these types of deals, we are always willing to work with like-minded entrepreneurs that want to collaborate.

## Summary

All of the strategies in this book will help you to grow a business, but they will take time and effort. So I would also focus on acquisitions, which are much less effort. If you want to double your sales organically, that's going to need a lot of marketing and change.

Alternatively, you could just buy a similar-sized competitor and overnight you'll have doubled your sales.

I am no longer involved in the day-to-day running of the companies I buy or invest in. This means I can focus my time on the areas of business that I am good at: finding and doing deals. If you want to build wealth through mergers and acquisitions, I strongly advise you to build a team around you who can take care of operations. Find people who are smarter than you. You can give them an equity stake so that they are aligned with the goals of the business and have a vested interest in sticking around and achieving them.

In terms of finding lenders and funders, this takes time and a lot of networking and meetings. Over time, we have built a suite of investors and lenders who understand us, our model and our track record, which means it's now fairly straightforward to organise funding.

## SEVEN
# Capital Markets And Wealth

While one surefire way to build wealth is buying and selling companies, the big money is in the capital markets. I have been involved in several public companies, but I will share the model for the vehicle we have now and how we use it to significantly increase value for shareholders and improve the companies we buy.

Listing a company is a time consuming and expensive thing to do, but once you get several deals under your belt, the wealth you create can pay for it. There are many different markets on which you can list, and this book won't get into too much detail, but you are typically looking at around £400–500k upfront to do it properly on a main market and then around 5% of whatever you raise (so if you raised £10m, you would need another £500k) generally contingent on raising the capital.

For most exchanges, the listing process is fairly straightforward, if time consuming, but it is a process. You must engage professional advisers including accountants, lawyers, listing agents and investment banks/market makers, who generally work on a fee basis that is not contingent (so if you don't list, you end up with the bill). Typically, you are looking at a six- to twelve-month process and while the application itself takes generally only a few weeks, there is a lot of work that goes into it before you start the application. Once complete, though, you have a PLC that you can use to raise more capital, or use the public shares as currency to do deals.

Before we get into the various different types of public listing, I want to share a unique model, Agglomeration™. This model was developed by Callum Laing, CEO and co-founder of MBH Corporation PLC, an investment company listed on both the Frankfurt and Düsseldorf Stock Exchanges and the OTCQX in New York, which acquires and invests in SMEs and helps them grow and scale, who has kindly agreed for me to share the following explanation, written specifically for this book.

## AGGLOMERATION™
## BY CALLUM LAING

If you want to start a new business, there is a wealth of information out there on how to launch your start-up. If you are an employee in a big corporate, there are countless books on every minutiae of each different department plus team building, management leadership, etc. Yet if you're a successful small business owner wondering what's next for your company, you will discover the bookshelves are practically empty.

Successful small businesses face a desert to cross if they are to make the leap from small and profitable to large and corporate. Without funding, which is nearly impossible to find outside of tech bubbles, the small business will find itself overlooked for the big contracts and unable to compete for the best talent against the deep pockets and perks of corporate life.

Unable to break through this glass ceiling, these businesses start to plateau. Plateauing for an entrepreneur is the same as going backwards. We are addicted to growth. Although by this stage the business owner is hopefully drawing a good salary and nice dividends in the good years, the time will come when they start to look around and ask, "What next?" Having put money back into the business one time too many, the business owner will eventually wake up with the feeling that everyone else seems to be making more money out of this venture than they are.

Clearly, if it is successful then a wide range of people are extracting value from the business: clients, employees, their families plus a whole ecosystem of suppliers, contractors, landlords etc. The economic footprint of a successful business reaches far and wide.

Typically, there is only one person who doesn't get to extract a commensurate amount of money from the business – the business owner. In fact, it tends to be quite the opposite; it is very easy to put money into a company, much harder to pull it back out again.

This is the trade-off we make as business owners. We create value for others and, at some distant point in the future, we will be rewarded for it. Yet as we get closer to that point, we discover our route to recapturing that value we provided to others is not so clear cut. No one is going to give us a suitcase full of cash to just walk away from the business. The typical exit remains having your company bought by a bigger player in the industry. A trade sale. The problem with this is that, for obvious reasons, most of these deals are structured as an earn out with the founder having to remain in the business and hit increasing targets over the coming years to earn their consideration.

This would be fine, but there is an inherent conflict. Entrepreneurs do not make good employees. We are just not good at being told what to do, especially when it comes to our own business. All too often, after six months, maybe a year, of trying to protect staff and clients from new overlords, the founder either quits or is fired from the new structure, often leaving a big chunk of the deal on the table.

The Agglomeration™ concept was built to solve this problem for small businesses and inadvertently ended up paving a new solution for investors too. In a nutshell, an agglomeration is simply a publicly listed holding company exclusively for the use of good, well-run, small businesses. Each company swaps their private stock for public stock yet retains full operational control of the business, brand, hiring and firing, their culture. The founder's compensation is structured on a perpetual earn-in model, meaning the more profit they contribute to the holding company, the more public stock they end up owning. This means they can leverage the balance sheet of the PLC to win bigger contracts. They can attract and retain staff using public stock options and they can even use the currency of the stock to make their own acquisitions.

You end up with a cooperative of business owners, heavily invested in their own success and the success of others that join the group. Investors often bemoan the fact that executives don't own stock in the companies they run, don't have a stake in its future, but that is clearly not the case with agglomeration. Shareholder value is created in three key ways:

- Earnings per share (EPS) accretive acquisitions – buying companies with stock at a lower multiple than the multiple the PLC is trading at.
- Organic growth – companies leveraging the balance sheet of the group to win bigger contracts.
- Synergies – the sharing of best practice and the aligned interests of all the business owners in the group creates a perfect environment for profitable joint ventures to thrive.

Although built from the bottom up to solve a problem for business owners, the Agglomeration™ model also solves a key issue for investors. Approximately 50% of the developed world's Gross Domestic Product (GDP)[19] comes from small business, about 90% of private sector employment.[20] And yet, until now, there was no financial product that allowed investors to access this space. Investing in a solitary small business was too risky and too illiquid and so the finance industry and small business world remained divided.

By creating a publicly listed holding company of well-run small businesses, we finally have a situation where we can start to reconnect the capital markets with the people who actually create value in the world. The finance world tends to assume that small businesses are small because they lack the know-how that comes with expensive MBAs. In fact, most small businesses are far more capital efficient than many larger companies, primarily because it is the owner's money at stake. Add to that the huge impact small businesses have in terms of job creation and the fact that small businesses often lead the way in supporting their local communities, and you start to appreciate the importance of supporting them.

Politicians will often parrot soundbites about how important small business is, but the reality is that small businesses are fragmented, they do not have the lobbying power of the big companies and, despite the huge impact on GDP, rarely have a voice in economic discussions. While politicians think up various new rules and regulations to try and address inequality in the world, the reality is that if small business owners were

---

19 'Exploring Business: The importance of small business to the US economy' (2010) https://open.lib.umn.edu/exploringbusiness/chapter/5-2-the-importance-of-small-business-to-the-u-s-economy/
20 L McGowan, 'Why supporting SMEs is essential to rebuilding the UK's economy', BCRS (2021) https://bcrs.org.uk/why-supporting-smes-is-essential-to-rebuilding-the-uks-economy

given a level playing field and the resources they need, they could grow, hire more people and solve many of the problems we face today. Entrepreneurs, by nature, are problem solvers.

## IPO vs direct listing

A company looking to raise interest-free capital from the public by listing its shares on a public exchange has two options, an IPO or a direct listing. With IPOs, the company uses the services of intermediaries called underwriters, who facilitate the process and charge a commission for their work. Companies that can't afford underwriting, don't want share dilution, or are avoiding lockup periods often choose the direct listing process, a less expensive option than an IPO, in which no new shares are created and only existing, outstanding shares are sold with no underwriters involved. Without an intermediary, however, there is no safety net ensuring the shares sell. Direct listings are also known as Direct Placements or Direct Public Offerings. In this process, the company sells shares directly to the public without help from intermediaries.

### Initial Public Offering

In an IPO, new company shares are created and underwritten by an intermediary. The underwriter works closely with the company throughout the IPO process, including deciding the initial offer price of the shares, helping with regulatory requirements, buying the available shares from the company and then selling them to investors via their distribution networks. These networks comprise investment banks, broker-dealers, mutual funds and insurance companies. Prior to the IPO, the company and its underwriter partake in what's known as a roadshow, in which the top executives present to institutional investors in order to drum up interest in purchasing the soon-to-be public stock. Gauging the interest received from network participants helps the underwriters set a realistic IPO price for the stock. Underwriters may also provide a guarantee of sale for a specified number of stocks at the initial price as well as purchase any excess.

The underwriter has two options for distributing shares to initial investors: book-building, in which shares can be awarded to investors of their choosing, or auctions, in which investors who are willing to bid above the offer price receive the shares. These auctions are rare, a most notable example being Google's IPO in 2004.

All of these services come at a cost. Underwriters charge a fee per share, which may range anywhere from 3% to 7%. This means that a notable portion of the capital raised through the IPO goes to compensate intermediaries. While the safety of an underwritten public listing may be the best choice for some companies, others see more benefits with a direct listing.

## Direct listing

Not all companies who want to do a public listing will have the resources to pay underwriters. Alternatively, they may not want to dilute existing shares by creating new ones, or may want to avoid lockup agreements. Companies with these concerns often choose to proceed by using the direct listing process (DLP), rather than an IPO. This is also known as direct placement or a direct public offering (DPO).

With a DLP, the business sells shares directly to the public without the help of any underwriters or intermediaries; there are no new shares issued and there is no lockup period. The existing investors, promoters and any employees already holding shares of the company can sell their shares directly to the public.

However, the zero to low-cost advantage also comes with certain risks for the company, which trickle down to investors. There is no support or guarantee for the share sale, no promotions, no safe long-term investors, no possibility of options like greenshoe and no defence by large shareholders against any volatility in the share price during and after the share listing. The greenshoe option is a provision in an underwriting agreement that grants the underwriter the right to sell investors more shares than originally planned by the issuer if the demand proves particularly strong.

Both those companies that opt for a DLP and those that undergo an IPO must publicly file a registration statement on Form S-1 (or another applicable registration form) with the Securities and Exchange Commission (SEC) at least fifteen days in advance of the launch.

Upon listing of the company's stock (whether through direct listing or an IPO), companies are subject to the reporting and governance requirements applicable to all publicly traded companies. The SEC requires all publicly traded companies to prepare and issue two disclosure-related annual reports, one that is sent to the SEC and one that is sent to the company's shareholders. These reports are referred to as 10-Ks.

## SPAC

A special purpose acquisition company (SPAC) is a company that has no commercial operations and is formed strictly to raise capital through an IPO or to acquire/merge with an existing company. MBH Corporation PLC started out life as a SPAC.

Also known as blank check companies, SPACs have been around for decades, but their popularity has soared in recent years. At the time of their IPOs, SPACs have no existing business operations or even stated targets for acquisition. Investors in SPACs can range from well-known private equity funds and celebrities to the general public. SPACs are generally formed by investors or sponsors with expertise in a particular industry or business sector, to pursue deals in that area. When creating a SPAC, the founders sometimes have at least one acquisition target in mind, but they don't identify that target so as to avoid extensive disclosures during the IPO process.

This is why they are called blank check companies. IPO investors typically have no idea about the company in which they will ultimately be investing. SPACs seek underwriters and institutional investors before offering shares to the public. The funds SPACs raise in an IPO are placed in an interest-bearing trust account. These funds cannot be disbursed except to complete an acquisition or to return the money to investors if the SPAC is liquidated. In some cases, some of the interest earned from the trust can serve as the SPAC's working capital. After an acquisition, a SPAC is usually listed on one of the major stock exchanges.

An investor in a SPAC IPO is making a leap of faith that its promoters will be successful in acquiring or merging with a suitable target company in the future. The reduced degree of oversight from regulators, coupled with a lack of disclosure from the typical SPAC, means that retail investors run the risk of being saddled with an investment that could be massively overhyped or occasionally even fraudulent.

SPAC IPOs raised $13.6bn in 2019, which was more than four times the $3.5bn they raised in 2016. But SPACs really took off in 2020 and 2021, with as much as $83.4bn being raised in 2020 and $162.5bn in 2021. As of March 2022, SPACs have raised $9.6bn. During this boom period for SPACs, they attracted big-name underwriters such as Goldman Sachs, Credit Suisse and Deutsche Bank, as well as retired or semi-retired senior executives. In addition, so many celebrities, including entertainers and professional sportspeople, became involved with SPACs that, in March 2021, the SEC issued an Investor Alert. It cautioned investors not to make investment decisions related to SPACs based solely on celebrity involvement.

One of the most high-profile SPAC deals involved Richard Branson's Virgin Galactic. Venture capitalist Chamath Palihapitiya's SPAC Social Capital Hedosophia Holdings bought a 49% stake in Virgin Galactic for $800m before listing the company in 2019. In 2020, Bill Ackman, founder of Pershing Square Capital Management, sponsored his own SPAC, Pershing Square Tontine Holdings, the largest ever SPAC, raising $4bn in its offering. As of February 2022, the SPAC has not been liquidated or de-listed.

In light of the potential difficulties and controversies, why would a company go public through a SPAC and not an IPO? Chiefly, to save time and money. A company acquired by a SPAC can go public in a matter of months, while the conventional IPO process is arduous and can take anywhere from six months to over a year, involving complex regulatory filings and months of negotiations with underwriters and regulators. This can deter a company's plans to become publicly listed, especially during periods of heightened uncertainty (such as the pandemic years), in which the risk of investors giving an IPO a frosty reception is much greater.

Indeed, the soaring popularity of SPACs in 2020 may be partly due to their shorter time frame for going public, as many companies chose to forego conventional IPOs due to the market volatility and uncertainty triggered by the global pandemic.

The owners of a target company may also be in a better position to negotiate a favourable price from a SPAC that has a limited time frame to make an acquisition, compared with another buyer like a private equity firm, which may drive a hard bargain. Being acquired by or merging with a SPAC that is sponsored by prominent financiers and business executives can also provide the target company with experienced management and enhanced market visibility. Some of the best-known companies to have become publicly listed by merging with a SPAC are digital sports entertainment and gaming company DraftKings; aerospace and space travel company Virgin Galactic; energy storage innovator QuantumScape; and real estate platform Opendoor Technologies.

What happens if a SPAC does not merge? SPACs usually have between eighteen and twenty-four months in which to merge with another company and close a deal. If a SPAC cannot merge during the allotted time, then it liquidates and all funds are returned to investors.

## Wealth

At the start of this book, I told you that 99% of people in developed countries follow a similar path: they complete their education, get a job, work for circa forty years for a salary, live their lives on debt (the car is leased, there is a mortgage to pay etc). Income is what you spend; the more you earn, the more you spend. Most people live to their means. Then you stop work and live off a pension, which isn't quite enough to make ends meet so you probably downsize, and with inflationary pressures, your pension doesn't quite meet the cost of living. Then you die. And as I said earlier, f*** that. If you want to be in the 1%, you need to create capital events and reinvest that capital into assets and passive income streams.

To reiterate, the biggest opportunity right now to create significant wealth is that 40% of SMEs are owned by baby boomers, the vast majority without an exit strategy.[21]

---

21  M Hall, 'Unsexy but thriving businesses: the hidden opportunity gifted to us by baby boomers', Forbes.com (25 January 2022) www.forbes.com/sites/markhall/2022/01/25/unsexy-but-thriving-businesses-the-hidden-opportunity-gifted-to-us-by-baby-boomers

## CAPITAL MARKETS AND WEALTH

If you trade businesses – buy businesses, improve them then sell them for a higher multiple than you paid, with that multiple applied to a higher profit (due to improvements you've made) – you earn a monthly fee from the business for your time and expertise, which pays for your day-to-day living. Then, when you exit, the capital you obtain you reinvest.

If, over the next five years, you buy and sell five companies (one a year), each of which is making £1m, and you pay £3m to acquire them (by raising debt and through seller financing) and you improve the profits in all of them to £1.5m by using the tactics in this book and sell them for a multiple of four (remember you bought at a multiple of three) your profit would look like this:

| 5 x Companies Making £1m | Bought for £3m | Cost: £15m |
| 5 x Companies Making £1.5m | Sold for £6m | Profit: £30m |

This gives you £30m to invest in income-producing assets like real estate, or structured products, gold, bonds, stocks, shares, ETFs, cryptocurrency etc. Your profit is £30m (rather than £15m) as you didn't put your own money into the deal in the first place.

### Private banking

Typically, the wealthy get wealthier, especially when you are wealthy enough to qualify for private banking. Private banking gives you access to experienced wealth bankers who know where to invest to get the returns. Obviously investments carry risk, some more than others, but if you diversify and invest sensibly then you can hedge this risk and, of course, you don't have to put all your eggs in one basket, not just in terms of what you invest in but in terms of the banks you choose to look after your money.

A further asset of wealth banking is Lombard lending. Lombard loans are loans the bank will give you against your portfolio. It's a bit like when you take out a mortgage against a property; you pledge the property to the bank as security and then pay the mortgage off over time. Lombard lending works similarly but you leverage liquid assets rather than property. You could put £1m in the bank in cash and the bank will lend you pretty much all of that back, so you keep £1m in the bank and then invest the other £1m to create returns. You can invest in the bank's products, for instance equities, bonds, commodities and structured products. Or you can withdraw the cash and invest it in deals, whether that be real estate or business acquisitions. You only have to pay the interest, not the capital, in repayments or roll the loan over if you haven't yet turned what you borrowed into more cash. This is how the wealthy get wealthier.

I have a diverse portfolio that I leave the expert banks to invest and reinvest profits from. Did you know there are some stocks that pay dividends every month? Cryptocurrency, while volatile, is part of my portfolio. I also have bonds that pay regular coupons. You get the gist.

## Selling a company

How do you sell a company? The first rule I have is: never deal with a broker. Anyone who acts as a middleman in selling a business, whether it be a broker or corporate adviser, charges fees, most of the time upfront. In my experience, to justify these fees they will over-value a business. Of course, a business is only worth what a willing buyer will pay, but I have found most brokers to be deal blockers rather than deal makers. I have heard business brokers brag that they make more money from the upfront fees they charge to list a business than from the commission on the sale.

I have sold many companies and I have found the best way to approach the process is to first get your house in order. By which I mean make sure all of your systems and processes are documented and your financials are up to date. A sign of a well-run business is that they can quickly produce an up-to-date profit and loss account and balance sheet. Second, make yourself redundant from the business. Ensure you have a top team and leader in the business. If you want to avoid lengthy earn outs and payment periods then you need to show that the business can operate without you; this reduces the risk for a buyer.

Third, write a long list of potential buyers; think customers, suppliers, competitors, related businesses (this could be a tactical acquisition for them because it will increase their margins). Fourth, write an information memorandum. You should have a short and a long version, with the short version (two or three pages) summarising the investment opportunity and business with some key financials (last three to five years' turnover, gross profit and EBITDA), and the longer version with more detail for those that are interested.

Finally, approach potential targets with your information memorandum. You may not want to do this directly, to protect confidentiality, but you can set up your own broker to act as a middleman, or you can retain a corporate adviser to approach potential buyers and put an NDA in place before discussions commence. I would do this on a fee basis so you just pay them to do the marketing, not act for you in the sale, for reasons previously mentioned.

Once you have a potential buyer interested you can provide a pre-populated data room of due diligence. In the appendix is a due diligence checklist of items that a buyer is likely to want to review. It's a bit like when you buy a house, you pay a solicitor to review the legal title and a surveyor to review the structure; buying a business is no different. Though there will (usually) only be one ultimate buyer, it's a good idea to have more than one horse in the race. This creates competitors and provides a plan B if the first buyer should pull out.

## Tax and citizenship

The US is the only country on the planet that taxes its citizens whether they live in the country or not. The only way out of this is to renounce your US citizenship; to do this, you would need to secure citizenship in another country.

There are some countries that do not have any income tax, such as the UAE. I believe in paying tax but I can choose to live in a lower tax jurisdiction. The US, UK and Australia are all high tax countries. Depending on your earnings, you can be taxed as much as 50%. There are countries in Europe with lower tax rates or that don't tax foreign gains or dividends, so you pay tax on local income but not on foreign income.[22]

Before World War One there were no passports. Now these documents are issued by every country in the world to their citizens. In some countries you can buy a passport and citizenship. In St Lucia, for example, you can buy citizenship for $100,000, which gives you visa-free travel to 146 countries (including Schengen countries, the UK, Hong Kong and Singapore) and means you can live in lower tax or no tax jurisdictions.

---

22  Look up Andrew Henderson, founder and CEO of Nomad Capitalist, if you want to learn more about this topic.

Some countries allow you to acquire citizenship by investing in real estate; for example, in Greece if you invest 250,000 euros you receive a golden visa giving you free access to travel, work and live in the EU.

This is not a debate about whether it's right or wrong to some, more or no tax. It's just telling you that, if you are prepared and able to move, you can set up a legal way to pay less tax.

Living in the country you were born in may not be the most tax-efficient option. If you think living in a warmer climate with lower taxes would allow you to live your best life, then it is possible.

## Summary

Going public, through an IPO or direct listing, is when business owners can feel they've 'made it', that their start-up has become a successful business. With this kind of success comes wealth, which opens up a whole new world of opportunities. It changes the landscape of the financing options that are open to you, and you can begin to live a very different kind of life, should you choose to. With wealth comes a new set of concerns – the global economic environment and future prospects, tax efficiency, even citizenship. With wealth also comes freedom – you can begin to think about what your 'best life' might look like.

# EIGHT
# The Way Forward

There is no right or wrong way in business. Everyone has their own style, but there are some fundamental things that tend to make businesses successful, some relative fail-safes. I'll talk you through some of these in this chapter.

## Real estate investing

When I started to create wealth to invest in real estate, my first thought was to do this locally to where I lived because I knew the area and property market, particularly as I had owned and worked in a real estate business for several years. But I've learned lessons and now know the importance of hiring an expert to deploy funds.

Before I moved to southern Europe, I had lived most of my life in England. The traditional buy-to-let market in the UK produces poor returns, usually about 4–5% per annum. It's also heavily regulated. Alternative opportunities in the UK residential market that produce better returns are HMOs (houses of multiple occupancy) such as student properties in university towns and cities, where it's not uncommon to achieve 10–15% returns. The downside of these is that they can be a pain in the backside to manage. Holiday rentals, particularly with the rise of Airbnb, can produce even better returns.

There are lots of commercial sale and leaseback opportunities. I've hived off property assets when I've acquired companies as separate investment vehicles. You can even package them up and sell them on; the annual return, the longer the lease, the better the tenant – these all influence the valuation.

Outside of the UK there are many emerging markets in which you can buy cheap real estate and generate excellent returns. Instead of an overheated London market, think Georgia, Belgrade, Montenegro, Malaysia, Dubai. You can pick up decent two-bedroom apartments for under £100,000 where there are hot rental markets and steady capital growth.

## KPIs

I must have spent an age with Excel spreadsheets devising key performance indicators. In my real estate business we track thirty-five KPIs, and in my recruitment business it's fifty-one. I have learned that in most businesses, there are four to six main KPIs to track; they must be simple and easy to measure and keep track of.

In my recruitment days, we could see how many jobs we had filled, how many candidates were registered, how many interviews we conducted, how many job offers closed, average fee, salary etc. This level of detail helped me identify problems. For example, if we were not closing many job offers, I would revisit that part of the process with my recruitment team to see what was going on. If we were not registering enough new clients, it was probably because we were not doing enough marketing calls, or the quality of those calls needed adjustment.

I don't think there is a right or wrong way; you can track four KPIs or forty. If you have lots, this helps identify problems; if you have a few, you can really focus on the key metrics. As an investor in businesses, I typically only track revenue, gross profit margin and EBITDA (earnings before interest, tax, depreciation and amortisation), which essentially amount to cash-flow generated. I compare to historic figures so I can see how we are improving.

Most senior executives running the businesses we are involved in typically tend to be measured on EBITDA and EBITDA growth and any financial rewards are linked to this. What gets measured gets delivered, and if you incentivise you have more chance of achieving your goals. If an executive has the chance to earn a big bonus for delivering a stretching target, they are going to strive harder to achieve it.

## Habits and actions

The biggest differentiator between those who succeed and those who don't achieve the levels of wealth they want, is habits and actions. I, my team and the partners I work with have one thing in common: we are all action takers. We get on with the task. But it is habits that create action.

Say you want to go on a diet to lose weight and exercise to get fitter. If you want to lose weight you need to consume a balanced diet and a limited number of calories a day. To get fitter, we need to exercise and/or go to the gym. But why do so many people fail when dieting? Because they don't create the habits that enable the bigger actions. For example, making sure the fridge is full of fresh fruit and vegetables, making a meal plan, putting an hour in the diary every day to do some exercise.

It's the same with deals. One of the ways we source acquisition opportunities is to write directly to shareholders of companies we like the look of. Every week, my team will send around 250 letters, a habit that gives us a regular flow of targeted acquisition opportunities.

## Making it

Since acquiring my first business, the nursery from my mother, I have been involved in many start-ups. My experience now tells me that the quickest way of 'making it' is to buy a business rather than start one. That being said, I do not regret my involvement in any start-ups, as they have taught me so much.

When you start a business and it is your name above the door and your neck on the line, you are the one kept awake at night with dilemmas like how to recruit better people, how to improve cashflow or how to get more customers. You have to find ways to solve these problems, and while they will exist in any business you acquire, in a start-up you are starting with nothing. It is a lot of fun starting a business but I rarely get involved in start-ups now. Since 2015, I have only invested in three, all of my other acquisitions being existing businesses. Yet while acquisitions are definitely the way forward, I would not have been able to acquire any businesses without my start up experience.

Having started businesses, and bought, sold and invested in many more, my conclusion is that the biggest opportunity to create wealth and a better life for you, your family and friends is to buy and sell companies, creating capital events that can be invested into income-producing assets. If an ambitious entrepreneur with a normal upbringing in England can do it, anyone can. I raise a glass to your rollercoaster ride – whether you are already on it, or are about to start.

If you have a business that you want to sell, are seeking investment to grow your company, or are already involved in mergers and acquisitions, why not get in touch and start a conversation? Nothing ventured, nothing gained.

# Acknowledgements

Writing *Buy, Build, Sell* has enabled me to reflect on the rollercoaster highs and lows of the past twenty-two years. There have been happy and fun times, as well as sad and challenging ones. Now, I have fond memories of those days, the deals I have done and the many brilliant people I have met, worked and done business with. There are too many to mention here, but I am grateful to all those who have made this life possible. You know who you are. I look forward to creating many more fun times – I'm not done yet.

# The Author

Paul Seabridge's business background began during his teenage years when he stepped in to sort out a family business that was losing money. Preferring to learn on the job rather than through academia, he went on to cut his teeth in real estate, quickly establishing himself as someone able to analyse strategic problems, identify opportunities and turn round companies to make them more efficient and more profitable.

A natural entrepreneur, he eventually realised he would rather work for himself than anyone else and has, over the past two decades, been involved in numerous business ventures covering a wide range of industries across the world. He is passionate about people – the core of any business – and continues to be excited by investments as well as mergers and acquisitions.

In this, his latest book, Paul shares his vast experience, business tips and commitment to wealth creation in the belief that, with a proactive mentality and can-do attitude, success is within anybody's grasp.

If you have a business opportunity that you think might interest Paul, get in touch with him:

🌐 www.opulentiacapital.com

in Opulentia Capital and Paul Seabridge

🐦 @seabrdg1

Printed in Great Britain
by Amazon